THE BEST
Flatiron
SCRAMBLES

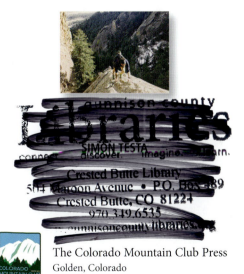

SIMON TESTA

The Colorado Mountain Club Press
Golden, Colorado

The Best Flatiron Scrambles
© 2020 by The Colorado Mountain Club

PUBLISHED BY

The Colorado Mountain Club Press
710 Tenth Street, Suite 200, Golden, Colorado 80401
303-996-2743   e-mail: cmcpress@cmc.org

Founded in 1912, The Colorado Mountain Club is the largest outdoor recreation, education, and conservation organization in the Rocky Mountains. Look for our books at your local bookstore or outdoor retailer or online at www.cmcpress.org/

Simon Testa: author, photographer, maps
Jodi Jennings: copyeditor
Sarah Gorecki: proofreader
Erika K. Arroyo: design and composition
Jeff Golden: publisher

CONTACTING THE PUBLISHER
We would appreciate it if readers would alert us to any errors or outdated information by contacting us at the address above.

DISTRIBUTED TO THE BOOK TRADE BY
Mountaineers Books, 1001 SW Klickitat Way, Suite 201, Seattle, WA 98134, 800-553-4453, www.mountaineersbooks.org

 Aerial imagery provided with permission from the Denver Regional Council of Governments Aerial Photography Project 2014.

 COVER PHOTO: John Sacco (foreground) and Aaron Stewart (background) scrambling Angel's Way, Ridge Three. Photo by Nicklaus Combs.

 We gratefully acknowledge the financial support of the people of Colorado through the Scientific and Cultural Facilities District of greater Denver for our publishing activities.

 Rocky Mountain Rescue Group relies on donations for a significant portion of its income and would like to thank the author for generously donating book proceeds to RMRG. RMRG is a nonprofit IRS 501(c)3 organization and it does not charge for its services. While RMRG supports the accurate dissemination of information on climbing and scrambling along with how to stay safe during these activities, the content of this book and views and opinions expressed are those of the author and not of RMRG. RMRG has not reviewed this publication and disclaims any associated liability.

WARNING: Although there has been an effort to make the scrambling and trailhead descriptions in this book as accurate as possible, some discrepancies may exist between the text and the routes in the field. Scrambling in mountainous and desert areas is a high-risk activity. This guidebook is not a substitute for your experience and common sense. The users of this guidebook assume full responsibility for their own safety. Weather, terrain conditions, and individual abilities must be considered before undertaking any of the hikes in this guide.

ISBN 978-1-937052-67-6
Printed in Korea

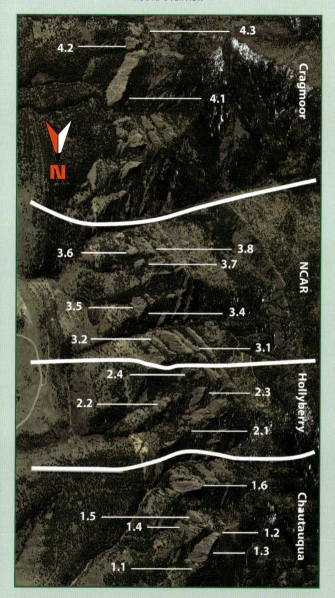

CONTENTS

Foreword

Bill Wright is a Boulder legend and one of the pioneers of scrambling on the Boulder Flatirons. Bill's enthusiasm and willingness to share his expansive Flatiron knowledge and wisdom have a lot to do with Flatiron scrambling increasing in popularity.

—Simon Testa

The Flatirons above Boulder, Colorado, are a truly unique climbing resource. You could almost say that about any classic climbing location—like Yosemite, the Gunks, or Eldorado Canyon—but the Flatirons, specifically the low-angled Ridges and East Faces, are unique in a much more fundamental way. Where else in the world, close to a major town, do people go out specifically to scramble? Nowhere. Where else can you do 1,000-foot scrambles on impeccable rock before work or during a long lunch? Nowhere. Pure rock climbers, interested primarily in gymnastic difficulty, would quickly overlook these formations. But for others, here lies a whole new realm of climbing: scrambling.

What is scrambling? Scrambling is easy, gently-angled rock climbing where one is comfortable without a rope. Technically, that means Class 3 climbing, but, depending on your experience and comfort with exposure and risk, this rating can creep upward into low 5th class. I differentiate scrambling from "soloing" mainly on the basis of steepness. If I'm never dependent upon my arms for more than a moment, then it is scrambling. Here I can take my time without any fear of getting pumped. I also refer to scrambling as "adventure hiking." I use these terms to minimize the bravado of "soloing" a rock climb, but it shouldn't be taken as a lack of respect for the danger involved.

Around Boulder scrambling is becoming more and more popular, hence Simon's excellent guidebook, **but beware**. While the climbers seen on these rocks make it look easy, here be dragons. People regularly get rescued off the Flatirons and occasionally fall to their deaths. **This is very serious business.** My recommendation is, whenever there is any doubt at all, to always climb the route first with a rope, gear, and a partner. Even climbing like that can be quite dangerous, as many of these routes don't offer a lot of protection opportunities. But first use a rope and climbing shoes and only then can you decide for yourself if the route is a reasonable scramble *for you*.

Having such bountiful rocks, so easily accessible, is one of the blessings of Boulder. Yet it took a serious climbing accident for me to really become a scrambler. I thought scrambling would be a quick stepping-stone on my road to recovery. Instead it has become a lifelong pursuit and, at times, an obsession. I've been incorporating scrambles into my trail runs for the last two decades. Getting to the scrambling is always such a relief, as it marks the end of the arduous uphill running (hiking these days). The movement, position, and views are outstanding, but by far the best part of scrambling is being able to share the experience with your companions. On normal rock climbs, you are separated from your partners by the rope. On scrambles, you are side-by-side the entire time. Conversation can flow or not, but sharing these rocks is a sublime experience.

Simon has done a masterful job on this guidebook. His choice of routes is stellar. His detailed descriptions will keep you from getting lost. **Now go get some Flatirons.**

—Bill Wright

Acknowledgments

Special thanks to the Colorado Mountain Club for publishing this guide and to the Denver Regional Council of Governments for allowing the use of its 2014 aerial imagery. Thanks to many for suggestions on the scrambles to include (or not) and particularly to Brian Crim for reviewing the content. Many thanks to those who contributed photos. Finally, I'm grateful for the great Front Range scrambling community and the many fantastic scrambling partners that have helped foster my love for scrambling on the Flatirons.

Disclaimer: Scrambling is dangerous and has the potential to result in serious injury or death. It is your sole responsibility to ensure that you scramble as safely as possible and within your abilities. By using this guide, you acknowledge that you scramble at your own risk and take responsibility for your own actions. The Colorado Mountain Club and its authors and contributors accept no liability for the actions of individuals based upon the information contained in this guide.

Dedication

I dedicate this guidebook to my family: my wife, Christin, and my daughters, Tilly and Eira, who are my favorite adventure partners.

Introduction

The Boulder Flatirons offer a high concentration of world-class scrambling on high-friction sandstone slabs, including routes longer than 1,000 feet. It is not surprising that Flatirons scrambling continues to increase in popularity. This guide aims to direct both new and veteran scramblers to the best-of-the-best Flatirons scrambles by providing detailed information for readers to make informed and safer decisions while travelling unroped on these moderate rock climbs.

Twenty-five scrambles and scramble link-ups are included. Over 20,000 feet of scramble-able rock is described, with individual scrambles and scramble link-ups varying in length from 200 feet (Sunnyside Two, Der Zerkle) to the longest link-up, the Flatirons Trifecta, which includes over 3,000 feet of scrambling.

This guide highlights what are, in the author's opinion, the best scrambling routes in the area. The routes were selected using the following criteria:

- technical climbing rating of 5.5 or less,
- high quality from both a rock quality and overall aesthetic appeal,
- short approach and uncomplicated and descent, and
- not requiring a rope for descent (with the exception of the East Face on the Third Flatiron). However, if a rappel is possible, it is described in the scramble description section.

Scrambling Season: Although more consistent conditions exist from early spring through the end of fall, the Flatirons can be typically scrambled during every month of the year.

Guide Format: This guide is designed to be easy-to-follow and to conveniently fit in a pocket or pack. It is divided into four sections based on the City of Boulder's Open Space and Mountain Parks (OSMP) official trailheads. Each trailhead section includes scramble and scramble link-up descriptions and contains information on the round-trip distance and elevation gain, scramble difficulty (class) and length, round-trip time, scramble difficulty ranking, and descent type. The scramble descriptions include details on the approach, scramble route and descent, as well as color photos showing the start of each route and route overviews using high-resolution aerial imagery. The aerial imagery overviews show the OSMP trails (green lines), access trails (blue lines), and scramble routes (red lines).

The round-trip times are estimates of the total time required, at a moderate pace, to complete the scramble trailhead-to-trailhead. The Flatiron slabs are typically inclined around 45 degrees, so scramble length is described as on-rock length (i.e., rope length equivalent). Scramble lengths and scramble section lengths are best estimates determined using desktop mapping software.

The approach descriptions are based on the designated trails identified on OSMP's web-based interactive Trail Map at https://maps.bouldercolorado.gov/osmp-trails.

The detailed scramble descriptions are the author's interpretation of the route. In a couple of cases, the original rock climbing route has been slightly modified to provide a better scrambling experience.

SCRAMBLING ESSENTIALS

One of the many appeals of scrambling is that it requires no technical climbing equipment, except for appropriate footwear. Below is a recommended list of gear and safety considerations for your scrambling adventures in the Boulder Flatirons.

1. Appropriate Footwear. The only equipment required for scrambling is suitable footwear. The type of footwear to wear while scrambling is a matter of personal preference; most scramblers either wear technical rock climbing shoes or approach shoes with climbing-specific sticky rubber soles.

2. Rappel Equipment. As described, all of the scrambles in this guide (apart from the East Face on the Third Flatiron) can be descended without a rope. In some cases, optional rappels are also possible. If you plan on rappelling, you must ensure that you have adequate experience to do so. You will need a harness, a rappel device and carabiner, a rope of suitable length, and possibly tubular webbing and rappel rings to leave behind to back-up an existing rappel anchor or to create a new one.

3. This Guidebook! Until you are familiar with the scrambles, it is recommended that you bring this guide with you. It is designed to be easy to follow and to conveniently fit in a pocket or pack. It contains all the needed information to get to the trailhead, approach the scramble, and ascend and descend.

4. Hydration. The type and volume of hydration is a matter of personal preference. Bringing plenty of water, particularly on the longer link-ups, is recommended.

5. Sustenance. Much like hydration, the type and volume of sustenance is a matter of personal preference. Bringing a snack or meal, particularly on the longer link-ups, is recommended.

6. Sun Protection. Colorado has many sunny days. Sunscreen helps to protect against the often intense Colorado sun.

7. Small Backpack. Many scramblers bring a small trail running-style backpack to carry their belongings.

8. Cell Phone. It is prudent to carry a cell phone in case of emergency.

9. High Socks. Poison ivy grows in the Flatirons and is often prevalent on the access trails. Know how to recognize and avoid it. Wearing high socks can also help mitigate getting poison ivy below the knee. Additionally, high socks can be useful for drying the base of your footwear before scrambling if they get wet or muddy during the approach.

10. Leave Behind Information. It is good practice to inform a family member or friend of your planned route and estimated time of return, so they can initiate a search and rescue if necessary.

Scrambling Etiquette: It is critical to act conscientiously around other scramblers and roped parties while on the rock. If you encounter unroped or roped parties moving at a slower pace, ALWAYS request their permission to pass before doing so.

Leave No Trace: The Boulder Flatirons are an incredible location for outdoor recreation and one of the best places in the country for scrambling. Help preserve, protect, and maintain access to this wonderful resource. Leave no trace, pack out what you pack in, follow OSMP rules and regulations, and refrain from cutting switchbacks.

Seasonal Closures: Boulder Open Space and Mountain Parks enforces cliff-nesting raptor closures for some Flatiron areas and rock formations. The closures typically occur from February 1 through July 31. Closure times and areas can vary from year to year, so consult OSMP's webpage to determine which closures are in effect: https://maps.bouldercolorado. gov/wildlife-closures.

Three of the scrambles described are typically subject to closure. These closures are identified in the scramble and scramble link-up sections and in the table below.

SEASONAL CLOSURES FOR RAPTOR NESTING	
Formation Name	**Route Name**
Third Flatiron	East Face
Ridge Three	Angel's Way
Der Freischutz	East Face Left

Rating System: The Yosemite Decimal System is used in this guide. Scrambles vary from Class 4 to 5.5. The class for an individual scramble represents the hardest move or crux. A class range is provided for all scramble link-ups, comprising the range in class of the included individual scrambles.

"Scramble" Defined: The term "scramble" is subjective; a scramble to one person may feel like a hike or a climb to another. However, it is widely accepted that scrambling refers to the transition between hiking and climbing, and this transition begins when one's hands are used. A distinction often made between scrambling and climbing is whether an ascent requires one's hands to pull up one's body weight (climbing), or just for balance and upward momentum (scrambling). Scrambling is accomplished without a rope or other climbing equipment.

Scrambling is typically reserved for routes with a difficulty of Class 3 or 4. This guide includes routes designated with technical climbing grades from 5.0 to 5.5, so arguably a more appropriate term for these grades is free soloing. But the low angle of the Flatirons (typically around 45 degrees) is the primary reason for describing these routes as scrambles. One's movement up Flatiron slabs is primarily driven by the feet, with hands used mainly for balance, security, and upward momentum. Some of the harder crux moves may require greater use of the hands and thus feel more like "climbing," but such moves are the exception, not the rule.

Seventy percent of the scrambling routes in this guide have a technical climbing grade of 5.0 or above. Many of these routes are exposed and have sustained sections of scrambling without convenient rests. The risk of death or serious injury is very high if one were to fall. If you are new to scrambling, it is recommended that you work your way through this guide from the easiest to the hardest scramble (refer to the Difficulty Ranking Section). And never hesitate to climb any route with a rope and belay before proceeding unroped.

Safety Thoughts: Scrambling allows for more freedom of movement and expeditious travel on rock than climbing with gear, but it involves the inherent risks of falling and potentially sustaining serious injury or death. It is always important to balance speed of travel with safety. SAFETY SHOULD ALWAYS BE FIRST.

Conditions in the Flatirons can rapidly change. Weather can worsen, holds can break, and more difficult terrain can be encountered if you stray off route. These risks are real. Always use your best judgment when using this guide.

Never scramble up anything you don't think you can scramble back down. If you find yourself in trouble or injured, try to stay calm and think clearly before acting. If you don't think you can safely extricate yourself from the situation, the best course of action is to call 911.

Difficulty Ranking: The scrambles described are listed in a suggested ranking of increasing difficulty to help guide readers on their journey through the Flatirons. The difficulty ranking considers scramble class, route finding and downclimbing difficulty, exposure, rock quality, ease of getting off route into more difficult terrain, and whether a route is sustained at the grade. Additionally, a **Top Pick** from each difficulty class is highlighted.

ROUTES INCLUDED IN THIS GUIDE

Rank	Formation	Route	Class
1	Der Zerkle	Sunnyside Two	4
2	Amoeboid	Buckets	4
3	**Second Flatiron**	**Freeway**	**4**
4	The Regency/ Royal Arch	El Camino Royale (Class 4 variation start)/ East Face	4
5	Northern Shanahan Crag	East Face	4
6	The Slab	Diagonal (Class 4 variation start)	4
7	Second Flatiron	Dodge Block	5.0
8	Overture/Der Freischutz	South Ridge/East Face Left	5.0
9	Hammerhead	Yodeling Moves	5.0
10	**Frontporch**	**East Face Center**	**5.0**
11	Central Shanahan Crag	Southeast Ridge	5.0
12	**Ridge Three**	**Angel's Way**	**5.1**
13	**First Flatironette/Spy**	**South Ridge/ East Ridge**	**5.2**
14	First Flatiron	Southwest Face	5.2
15	Ridge One	Stairway to Heaven	5.3
16	First Flatiron	North Arête	5.3
17	**Third Flatiron**	**East Face**	**5.3**
18	Frontporch	Tiptoe Slab	5.3
19	**Dinosaur Rock**	**East Face/West Face**	**5.4**
20	**Fifth Flatiron**	**East Face South Side**	**5.5**

1.1 South Ridge / East Ridge
1.2 Southwest Face
1.3 North Arete
1.4 Freeway
1.5 Dodge Block
1.6 East Face

First Flatironette / Spy

First Flatiron

Second Flatiron

Third Flatiron

1.1
1.2
1.3
1.4
1.5
1.6

CHAUTAUQUA TRAILHEAD

COMMENT: The six scrambles and one scramble link-up in this section start at the Chautauqua Trailhead and cover over 7,400 feet of scrambling, including scrambles on the iconic First, Second, and Third Flatirons and an excellent scramble that combines the First Flatironette and Spy formations.

The Flatiron Trifecta link-up is a mega classic and includes over 3,000 feet of some of the best scrambling the Flatirons have to offer. The Third Flatiron is the only formation described in this guide that requires a rappel to descend.

Nicklaus Combs on East Ridge, Spy.   PHOTO BY SIMON TESTA

Refer to the Chautauqua Trailhead Overview map for the location of the individual scrambles.

GETTING THERE: To reach the Chautauqua Trailhead, turn west on Baseline Road at the intersection of Broadway and Baseline Road. Follow Baseline Road for 1.0 mile and turn left on Kinnikinic Road (Chautauqua Park entrance). Parking is available in the parking lot immediately on the right, around Chautauqua Park, or along Baseline Road and its side streets.

At the time of this guidebook's publication, the City of Boulder is charging a parking fee at Chautauqua and nearby neighborhood streets during summer weekends and holidays. The City is also providing free satellite parking and free shuttle service to and from Chautauqua. For more information on this program visit, https://bouldercolorado.gov/transportation/parktopark.

Angela Tomczik on East Face, Third Flatiron.　　PHOTO BY JENNY NICHOLS

1.1 South Ridge, First Flatironette and East Ridge, Spy

ROUND-TRIP DISTANCE	2.0 miles
ELEVATION GAIN	1,190 feet
CLASS	5.2
SCRAMBLE LENGTH	630 feet
ROUND-TRIP TIME	1 hour 30 minutes
DIFFICULTY RANK	13 of 20
DESCENT	Easy jump

COMMENT: The East Ridge of the Spy is a spectacular ridge that is less than 10 feet wide in places. As such, the Spy feels more exposed and committing than the First Flatironette, but both routes are mostly Class 4 with very short cruxy sections. This scramble offers excellent views of the First Flatiron's spectacular East Face.

APPROACH: From the Chautauqua Trailhead, head west (toward the Flatirons) on the Chautauqua Trail for 0.65 mile to the junction with the Bluebell-Baird and the Flatirons Loop trails. Head straight and uphill on the Flatirons Loop Trail for 0.1 mile and then turn right onto the 1st/2nd Flatiron Trail. Continue 0.2 mile on the 1st/2nd Flatirons Trail and take the Spy Climbing Access Trail on the right. You can see the base of the First Flatironette from the Spy Climbing Access Trail junction. Continue 30 yards to the base of the First Flatironette (photo 1.1.1).

SCRAMBLE: Start the scramble close to the lower left side of the formation (photo 1.1.1). Initially trend right (north) around

Photo 1.1.1. Start of South Ridge.   PHOTO BY SIMON TESTA

a steeper section and then up and left (south) to intersect the south ridge. Follow the ridge to the top of the first piece of the rock. Step onto the next piece of rock and climb a short steep wall. Make an awkward downclimb (5.0) into a notch between this and the next piece of rock. The first 200 feet to this point are Class 4. The next piece of rock is the main section of the First Flatironette and has some 5.1 moves. Head straight up, staying left of a vertical groove and following a shallow vertical crack system. Then trend up and right and step onto the next piece of rock. Continue heading up, staying on the left edge of the ridge. Scramble up the final piece of rock to reach the southern summit, after just over 400 feet in total.

Downclimb (Class 3) a few feet and then walk north until you reach the Spy formation (escape is possible from here by walking up and west along the southern edge of the Spy).

Photo 1.1.2. Simon Testa on Spy Jump descent viewed from the south.

PHOTO BY NICKLAUS COMBS

Head down (east) next to the southern edge of the Spy until you can walk no farther. At this point, gain the Spy's East Ridge at a step using good holds on its south side (5.0). Due to the Spy's narrowness, the upward path is apparent. Climb about 100 feet to a bulge. The bulge is above a miniature tree and is the route's crux (5.2). The crux is short, and the climbing then eases in difficulty. Reach a false summit after another 100 feet. From here, scramble down and west and then climb a short slab to the final summit.

From the left end of the summit make an easy jump across a gap to another rock (photo 1.1.2). After the jump, cross a rock band and hike down (east) along the Spy's northern edge to the Spy Climbing Access Trail. The access trail starts where a rocky ridge comes in from the left. Follow the access trail past the base of the First Flatironette to the 1st/2nd Flatiron Trail. From here, retrace the approach route to the Chautauqua Trailhead.

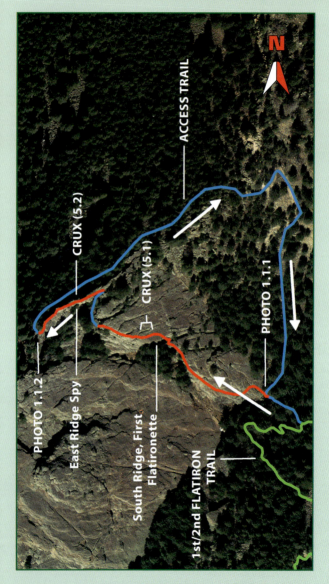

ACCESS TRAIL

N

CRUX (5.2)

CRUX (5.1)

PHOTO 1.1.1

PHOTO 1.1.2

East Ridge Spy

South Ridge, First Flatironette

1st/2nd FLATIRON TRAIL

1.2 Southwest Face, First Flatiron

ROUND-TRIP DISTANCE	2.5 miles
ELEVATION GAIN	1,510 feet
CLASS	5.2
SCRAMBLE LENGTH	400 feet (up and down)
ROUND-TRIP TIME	1 hour 40 minutes
DIFFICULTY RANK	14 of 20
DESCENT	Downclimb (5.2) or rappel

COMMENT: The Southwest Face is included here primarily as a descent route for the North Arête (Section 1.3), but it is a fun upward scramble too and is the easiest and shortest route to the First Flatiron's impressive summit. Because the route's upper section is steep and exposed, it's a good idea to scramble up it before scrambling down it for the first time. This route is steeper than the typical Flatirons scramble, but the handholds are large and plentiful. It is possible to rappel west from the First Flatiron's summit anchors, but here reversing the Southwest Face is described as the descent.

APPROACH: From the Chautauqua Trailhead, head west (toward the Flatirons) on the Chautauqua Trail for 0.65 mile to the junction with the Bluebell-Baird and the Flatirons Loop trails. Head straight and uphill on the Flatirons Loop Trail for 0.1 mile and then turn right onto the 1st/2nd Flatiron Trail. Continue 0.8 mile on the 1st/2nd Flatirons Trail, past where the trail passes close to the top of the Second Flatiron and then up some short switchbacks to an access trail on the right that leads to the Southwest Face (photo 1.2.1).

SCRAMBLE: Start the scramble behind a log (photo 1.2.1). Climb steeply and slightly right. After 20 feet, reach a ramp with a roof that heads diagonally up to the left. Follow this a short way, turn 180 degrees at the ramp's end, and find a small step and a short steep wall to reach the next ramp system up. The scrambling is steep, but the handholds are large and plentiful. Follow the path of least resistance along the ledge/ramp system. After 145 feet from the start, there is a large ledge/bowl with a rappel anchor. From here, continue up an easy ramp to the base of the steep 25-foot west face

Log

Photo 1.2.1. Pete Fox on start of Southwest, First Flatiron.

THE BEST FLATIRON SCRAMBLES

Photo 1.2.2. Pete Fox on start of Southwest Face Downclimb.

that leads to the summit. Climb the steep and exposed wall on good holds and then trend right to reach the summit.

To descend, reverse the route. It is also possible to rappel west, with a single 60-meter rope, from the summit anchors. Photo 1.2.2 shows the start of the downclimb. At the base of the scramble, retrace the approach route to the Chautauqua Trailhead.

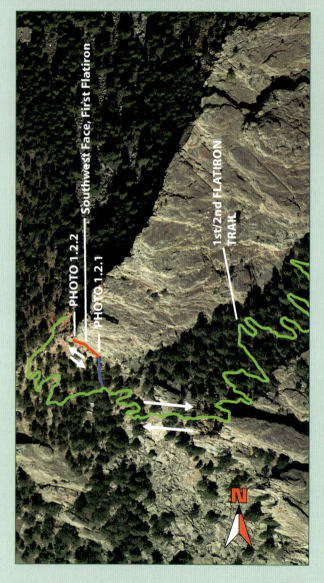

Southwest Face, First Flatiron

PHOTO 1.2.2

PHOTO 1.2.1

1st/2nd FLATIRON TRAIL

N

1.3 North Arête, First Flatiron

ROUND-TRIP DISTANCE	2.4 miles
ELEVATION GAIN	1,510 feet
CLASS	5.3
SCRAMBLE LENGTH	850 feet
ROUND-TRIP TIME	1 hour 50 minutes
DIFFICULTY RANK	16 of 20
DESCENT	Downclimb Southwest Face (5.2) or rappel

COMMENT: The North Arête is a 650-foot ridge and one of the most impressive scrambles in the Flatirons. Most of this classic scramble is Class 4, but it includes a few steeper and exposed crux sections up to 5.3. It is possible to rappel west from the summit anchors, but here the 200-foot Southwest Face (Section 1.2) is described as the downclimb, making this scramble 850 feet.

APPROACH: From the Chautauqua Trailhead, head west (toward the Flatirons) on the Chautauqua Trail for 0.65 mile to the junction with the Bluebell-Baird and the Flatirons Loop trails. Head straight and uphill on the Flatirons Loop Trail for 0.1 mile and then turn right onto the 1st/2nd Flatiron Trail. Continue 0.2 mile on the 1st/2nd Flatirons Trail and take the Spy Climbing Access Trail on the right. Follow the Spy Climbing Access Trail for 0.1 mile north past the base of the First Flatironette and then west 0.1 mile up along the north side of the Spy formation. When the Spy formation ends, continue uphill for 90 yards along the north side of the First Flatiron. Gain the scramble at a notch that is the last place for the arête to be reached easily (photo 1.3.1).

SCRAMBLE: Gain the arête by climbing a 20-foot steep section (photo 1.3.1). Follow the arête for 650 feet to the summit, never straying far from the arête proper. Along the way, there are three cruxes. The first, after 130 feet, is the crux of the route (5.3) and has a small overhang managed by stepping left and up (photo 1.3.2). The crux move is exposed and a little awkward (look for a useful slotted side-pull for your right hand). The second crux section (5.2) is located after

Photo 1.3.1. Pete Fox on start of North Arête.   PHOTO BY SIMON TESTA

Crux

Photo 1.3.2. Pete Fox heading toward the crux on North Arête (5.3).
PHOTO BY SIMON TESTA

another 170 feet. This steeper section has an interesting large quartz crystal. The third (5.2) crux is 120 feet farther and is exposed and slabbly; two obvious options are possible here, straight up, or left and up. Left and up is easier. To gain the final summit, head up a small ramp on the right.

To descend, downclimb the Southwest Face (Section 1.2). It is also possible to rappel west, with a single 60-meter rope, from the summit bolts.

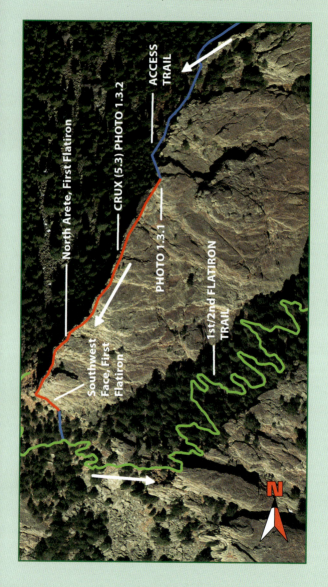

North Arete, First Flatiron

CRUX (5.3) PHOTO 1.3.2

ACCESS TRAIL

PHOTO 1.3.1

1st/2nd FLATIRON TRAIL

Southwest Face, First Flatiron

N

1.4 Freeway, Second Flatiron

ROUND-TRIP DISTANCE	2.3 miles
ELEVATION GAIN	1,330 feet
CLASS	4
SCRAMBLE LENGTH	800 feet
ROUND-TRIP TIME	1 hour 45 minutes
DIFFICULTY RANK	3 of 20
DESCENT	Downclimb (Class 3)

COMMENT: Freeway is a very popular Class 4 scramble that features the often-photographed jump from one slab to another. This classic 800-foot route is likely the most scrambled route in the Flatirons. It's popular because OSMP's trails run directly past the start and finish of the route, so it's easy to access. Also, the Second Flatiron's east face offers many variations that are straightforward at Class 4.

APPROACH: From the Chautauqua Trailhead, head west (toward the Flatirons) on the Chautauqua Trail for 0.65 mile to the junction with the Bluebell-Baird and the Flatirons Loop trails. Head straight and uphill on the Flatirons Loop Trail for 0.1 mile and pass the junction with the 1st/2nd Flatiron Trail on the right. Stay straight on the Flatirons Loop Trail and continue another 0.2 mile to the base of the Second Flatiron (photo 1.4.1).

SCRAMBLE: Start the scramble at the lowest point of the formation and head directly up 50 feet to a small bulge with a crack (photo 1.4.1). The bulge is hard Class 4 and the route's crux. After gaining the bulge, continue up for 160 feet to a right-facing corner system above a ledge. Scramble the corner system and make a couple of hard moves to reach

Bulge

Photo 1.4.1. Start of Freeway.

a tree. Continue up the corner system for 140 feet, past the tree, to the intersection with the south ridge of this part of the formation. Continue up the ridge for 220 feet to a small summit with a gap to the next slab. Jump across the gap from the apex of the small summit, or downclimb at a notch on the left. Continue up a slab for 160 feet, avoiding a small overhang on its right, to a second summit. Escape the second summit by stepping down to a ramp just right of the summit apex. Step across, via a boulder, to a 50-foot final face. Climb this, past a small tree, to the Freeway summit (this is not the summit of the Second Flatiron).

From here an easy downclimb past a tree (Class 3) takes you directly to the 1st/2nd Flatiron Trail. Descend the 1st/2nd Flatiron Trail for 0.6 mile to the junction with the Flatirons Loop Trail. From here, turn left on the Flatirons Loop Trail and retrace the approach route to the Chautauqua Trailhead.

Note that there is also a 5.2 West Face Route to the summit of the Second Flatiron, which is not included in this guide due to its lower quality.

1st/2nd FLATIRON TRAIL

FLATIRONS LOOP TRAIL

Freeway, Second Flatiron

CRUX (hard Class 4)

PHOTO 1.4.1

N

1.5 Dodge Block, Second Flatiron

ROUND-TRIP DISTANCE	2.3 miles
ELEVATION GAIN	1,330 feet
CLASS	5.0
SCRAMBLE LENGTH	750 feet
ROUND-TRIP TIME	1 hour 55 minutes
DIFFICULTY RANK	7 of 20
DESCENT	Walk off

COMMENT: Dodge Block is a great 750-foot scramble and a good alternative to the popular Freeway route for ascending the Second Flatiron. This classic route is varied and interesting as it tackles an unlikely overhang on the Second Flatironette, an enjoyable narrow rib on the Second Flatiron proper, and a surprising traverse across a steeper section to dodge the large overhanging Pullman Car.

APPROACH: From the Chautauqua Trailhead, head west (toward the Flatirons) on the Chautauqua Trail for 0.65 mile to the junction with the Bluebell-Baird and the Flatirons Loop trails. Head straight and uphill on the Flatirons Loop Trail for 0.1 mile and pass the junction with the 1st/2nd Flatiron Trail on the right. Stay on the Flatirons Loop Trail and continue another 0.2 mile until you reach the base of the Second Flatiron. From here, go around a large boulder next to the left side of the base of the east face of the Second Flatiron and follow an access trail up the drainage. The access trail jogs a couple of times to avoid the steeper sections of the drainage. The Second Flatironette is the next piece of rock, notable for its large overhang at 180 feet. The scramble starts on the left edge of the Second Flatironette (photo 1.5.1).

Photo 1.5.1. Mark Chaffee on start of Dodge Block.

PHOTO BY SIMON TESTA

SCRAMBLE: Gain the rock (photo 1.5.1) and head straight up the left (southern) edge of the Second Flatironette, passing a small step, toward the overhang. Stem up the weakness in the overhang and continue 250 feet to the summit of the Second Flatironette. Descend from the Second Flatironette just down and left of its summit. Head back east, down a short ramp, to an area below an obvious water groove. Locate a tree, and from behind it, scramble up a narrow rib just right of the groove. Head up the rib for 210 feet to its end at a very small summit. Continue straight to the next narrow rib and scramble up 80 feet. From here, continue up a right-facing corner until you are level with the last small tree in the groove to the right and about 30 feet below where the groove steepens significantly. Traverse right and down, and then climb a steep wall to dodge the overhang (photo 1.5.2).

Photo 1.5.2. Pete Fox approaching "The Dodge" on Dodge Block.
PHOTO BY SIMON TESTA

From here, follow a short ramp to a gully with trees. Follow the gully to the 1st/2nd Flatiron Trail (this route ends at the same place as Freeway and does not end on the summit of the Second Flatiron). Descend the 1st/2nd Flatiron Trail for 0.6 mile to the junction with the Flatirons Loop Trail. From here, turn left on the Flatirons Loop Trail and retrace the approach route to the Chautauqua Trailhead.

Note that there is also a 5.2 West Face Route to the summit of the Second Flatiron, which is not included in this guide due to its lower quality.

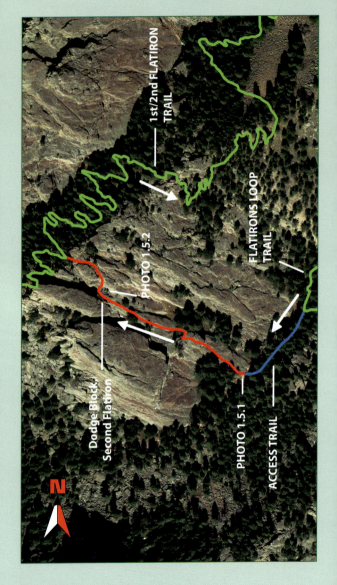

1st/2nd FLATIRON TRAIL

FLATIRONS LOOP TRAIL

PHOTO 1.5.2

Dodge Block, Second Flatiron

PHOTO 1.5.1

ACCESS TRAIL

N

1.6 East Face, Third Flatiron

SEASONAL CLOSURE	February 1 to July 31 (see page 12)
ROUND-TRIP DISTANCE	2.9 miles
ELEVATION GAIN	1,540 feet
CLASS	5.3
SCRAMBLE LENGTH	950 feet
ROUND-TRIP TIME	2 hours 20 minutes
DIFFICULTY RANK	17 of 20
DESCENT	Multiple rappels

COMMENT: The East Face of the Third Flatiron is one of the most iconic routes in the Flatirons. It is typically only open six months of the year due to a cliff-nesting raptor closure. The route is mostly Class 4, with a 5.2 move across a gully near the beginning of the route and a 5.3 slab to gain the summit. This is the only scramble described that requires rappels to descend. While a downclimb is possible via the 5.4 Southwest Chimney route, it is more serious than the other scrambles in this guide and thus is not described.

APPROACH: From the Chautauqua Trailhead, head south on Bluebell Road for 0.6 mile to the composting toilets. Continue on Bluebell Road for 300 yards to the junction with the Royal Arch Trail. Take the Royal Arch Trail 0.2 mile to where the Flatirons Loop Trail joins on the right. Turn onto the Flatirons Loop Trail and follow it for 0.2 mile. Turn left onto the Third Flatiron Climbing Access Trail and continue for 0.2 mile to the base of the East Face route at a ledge/bench (photo 1.6.1).

Photo 1.6.1. Pete Fox on start of East Face.

PHOTO BY SIMON TESTA

SCRAMBLE: This classic scramble follows a route past six fixed eyebolts on the east face. Toward the top of the east face you'll see the remnants of the giant painted letters C and U. The scramble crosses part of the letter C.

Start the scramble from the ledge/bench (photo 1.6.1). Head straight up for 10 feet and then traverse 15 feet left on good footholds to a diagonal weakness, passing the first eyebolt. Continue up 10 feet to the easiest place to cross a water-polished gully to the left (5.2). Cross, but do not climb, the water-polished gully. Scramble a short steep section up and left to gain the face of the rib left of the gully. Head straight up the rib for 30 feet to the next eyebolt. Continue up for several hundred feet to reach the sixth bolt by following the path of least resistance, including staying left of the third eye-bolt. Depending on your route, you may or may not spot the fourth and fifth eye-bolt, but in this area you'll cross a portion of the letter C. Continue up and slightly right past the sixth eye-bolt (you may not see this) near the upper right part of the letter C. A large gash in the face is just to the right. Stay left of the gash and angle slightly left to overcome a short steep section on great holds. Continue up the face and along flakes to a ledge next to a boulder wedged in the gash. Here, traverse across the gash to a two-foot ledge. Head right and along the ledge for 15 feet and then head up the slab above to a horizontal crack. Step left on the crack and finish up the left side of the exposed crux slab (5.3) to the summit.

From the summit, do three rappels from fixed anchors to reach the ground. First, rappel 48 feet south into a bowl from the summit anchors. Find the next set of fixed anchors on a large boulder and rappel 56 feet to an exposed ledge, **being careful to not rappel past the ledge**. There are two separate rappel anchors on this ledge; **do not use the first, single eyebolt anchor, as this is a 140-foot rappel!** Above the single eyebolt is a warning sign stating the rappel length from each of anchors on the ledge. Additionally, each anchor has a circular metal information tag around eyebolts. **Pay close attention** to continue west (climber's left) 10-feet past the first anchor and rappel 72 feet to the west from the second anchors. After rappelling, scramble (Class 3) a short way down to the west and then hike right (north) to join the Third Flatiron Climbing Access Trail. Follow the access trail down for 300 yards to the access trail taken on the approach. Turn left and retrace the approach to the Chautauqua Trailhead.

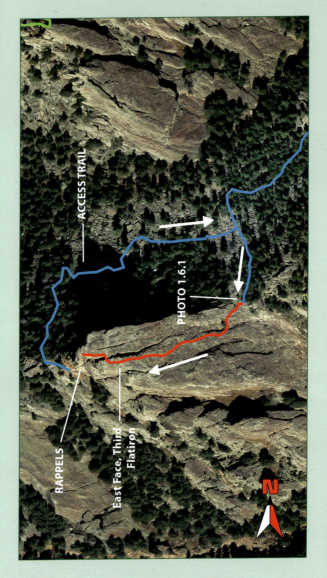

ACCESS TRAIL

PHOTO 1.6.1

RAPPELS

East Face, Third Flatiron

N

1.7 Flatirons Trifecta Link-up

SEASONAL CLOSURE	February 1 to July 31 (see page 12)
ROUND-TRIP DISTANCE	3.6 miles
ELEVATION GAIN	2,780 feet
CLASS	4 to 5.3
SCRAMBLE LENGTH	3,030 feet
ROUND-TRIP TIME	3 hours 30 minutes
DESCENT	Refer to individual scrambles

LINK-UP			
FORMATIONS	**ROUTES**	**CLASS**	**SCRAMBLE LENGTH**
Second Flatiron	Freeway	4	800 feet
First Flatironette/ Spy	South Ridge/ East Ridge	5.2	630 feet
First Flatiron	North Arête	5.3	850 feet
Third Flatiron	East Face	5.3	950 feet

COMMENT: There are many variations of what locals refer to as the "Flatirons Trifecta." The Trifecta typically comprises a combination of routes on the iconic First, Second, and Third Flatirons. This 3,030-foot variant (the longest link-up in the guide) also includes the First Flatironette and Spy formations and is Flatiron scrambling at its absolute best. The Third Flatiron scramble in this guide requires a rope to descend. As you will be carrying a rope, a rappel is also described in this link-up to descend the First Flatiron. Alternatively, the 5.2 Southwest Face of the First Flatiron (Section 1.2) can be downclimbed, which adds 200 feet to this link-up. Refer to the section overview map for the location of the individual scrambles.

APPROACH: Follow the approach for Freeway (Section 1.4).

SCRAMBLE: Start by following the description for Freeway (Section 1.4). After descending from Freeway, head down the 1st/2nd Flatirons Trail for 0.5 mile to the Spy Climbing Access Trail that joins on the left. Continue 30 yards on the Spy Climbing Access Trail to the base of the First Flatironette. From here, follow the First Flatironette/Spy description (Section 1.1). After the jump descent from the Spy, continue uphill for 90 yards along the north side of the First Flatiron. Gain the North Arête at a notch that is the last place that the arête can be reached easily. From here follow the North Arête description (Section 1.3).

From the summit of the First Flatiron, rappel west, with a single 60-meter rope, from the summit bolts. Alternatively, downclimb the Southwest Face (Section 1.2). From the base of the rappel, head southwest toward an obvious rock formation, the Sunset Flatironette, and follow an access trail near its east side, heading down (southeast). Turn left (downward) onto another access trail and head downhill for 100 yards to the Third Flatiron Access Trail. (It's about 0.2 miles from the start of the access trail to the Third Flatiron Access Trail.) Turn right and reach the start of the East Face after 70 yards. From here, follow the East Face description (Section 1.6).

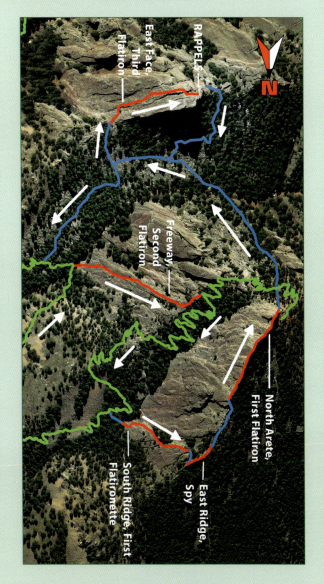

RAPPELS

East Face, Third Flatiron

Freeway, Second Flatiron

North Arete, First Flatiron

East Ridge, Spy

South Ridge, First Flatironette

First Flatiron Southwest Face downclimb.

THE BEST FLATIRON SCRAMBLES

HOLLYBERRY TRAILHEAD

COMMENT: The four scrambles and one scramble link-up in this section leave from the Hollyberry Trailhead and include 3,400 feet of scrambling. The scrambles include the second easiest (Buckets, Class 4) and the hardest (East Face South Side, 5.5) routes in the guide. The described link-up tours the Regency, Royal Arch, and Hammerhead formations, resulting in an excellent 1,300-foot tour with the difficulty never surpassing 5.0. Refer to the Hollyberry Trailhead Overview map for the location of the individual scrambles.

Simon Testa and Martin Le Roux on Buckets, Amoeboid.
PHOTO BY NICKLAUS COMBS

GETTING THERE: To reach the Hollyberry Trailhead, turn west on Table Mesa Drive from the intersection of Broadway and Table Mesa Drive. Follow Table Mesa Drive for 0.3 mile and turn right onto Gillaspie Drive. Follow Gillaspie Drive for 0.2 mile and turn left on Stanford Avenue. Continue straight for 0.4 mile where Stanford Avenue turns into Kohler Drive. After 0.6 mile, Kohler Drive ends at Hollyberry Lane. Turn right on Hollyberry Lane. Parking is available on the street near where the road bends to the right in about 100 yards.

John Christie on Hammerhead.   PHOTO BY KEVIN SMITH

Amoeboid

2.4

2.3

Fifth
Flatiron

2.2

The
Regency
/Royal
Arch

2.1

Hammerhead

2.1 Yodeling Moves
2.2 El Camino Royale/East Face
2.3 East Face South Side
2.4 Buckets

2.1 Yodeling Moves, Hammerhead

ROUND-TRIP DISTANCE	3.2 miles
ELEVATION GAIN	1,300 feet
CLASS	5.0
SCRAMBLE LENGTH	400 feet
ROUND-TRIP TIME	1 hour 50 minutes
DIFFICULTY RANK	9 of 20
DESCENT	Downclimb (5.0)

COMMENT: Yodeling Moves is a high-quality 400-foot scramble. This classic 5.0 route has two sections; a wonderful east ridge, followed by a steep rising traverse on a west face. The view of the Royal Arch to the south from the summit block is spectacular.

APPROACH: From the Hollyberry Trailhead, take the right-hand trail (Skunk Connector Trail) at the trail fork. Follow this northwest for 300 yards to the Skunk Canyon Trail. Turn left onto the Skunk Canyon Trail and follow it for 0.4 mile to the junction with the Skunk Canyon Spur Trail. Turn right onto the Skunk Canyon Spur Trail. After 0.1 mile, at a junction, turn left to stay on the Spur Trail. After 0.1 mile turn left onto the Kohler Mesa Trail and continue 0.4 mile to where it ends at the Mesa Trail. Turn right onto the Mesa Trail and then immediately left onto the Woods Quarry Trail. Follow the Woods Quarry Trail for 240 yards to an intersection. Turn left toward Woods Quarry and at the far southern end of the quarry, head uphill on an access trail. After 0.2 mile the access trail meets the Royal Arch Trail at a wooden fence. Turn left on the Royal Arch Trail and after 20 yards, leave the trail at a large rectangu-

Photo 2.1.1. Start of Yodeling Moves.   PHOTO BY SIMON TESTA

lar boulder and head uphill for 25 yards to the base of the Hammerhead (photo 2.1.1).

SCRAMBLE: Start the scramble just up and right of the base of the rock (photo 2.1.1). Scramble up and then traverse left to gain the east ridge. Follow an obvious weakness upward to a small pine tree at 130 feet from the start. Head up the face to the left, staying on the path of least resistance on the right side of the face. Reach a diagonal ledge after 25 feet. Head up the ledge to its left end and then straight up a vertical crack between two pieces of the formation The crack ends as it reaches the left edge of the piece of rock above. Follow the left edge of the rock to the summit. Toward the top the scrambling is a little steeper and there is a short slabby section. Downclimb a few feet from the summit and head through a gap/slot in rocks to the ground (escape is possible here by following the descent route to Sentinel Pass). Gain

Photo 2.1.2. Simon Testa on steep traverse to summit of Yodeling Moves, Hammerhead.

PHOTO BY NICKLAUS COMBS

the west face via a boulder wedged above the ground between the Hammerhead and another larger boulder. Make a steep and exposed 70-foot rising traverse to the flat summit of the Hammerhead on great in-cut handholds (photo 2.1.2).

To descend, reverse the traverse back to the ground. From here, hike downslope, staying close to the northern edge of the Hammerhead on an access trail. When you reach boulders, hike through a gap on the left and down the north side of the boulders to reach Sentinel Pass on the Royal Arch Trail 100 yards from the top of the scramble. Turn right on the Royal Arch Trail and continue for 100 yards back to the wooden fence. Turn left onto the access trail to the Woods Quarry and retrace the approach to the Hollyberry Trailhead.

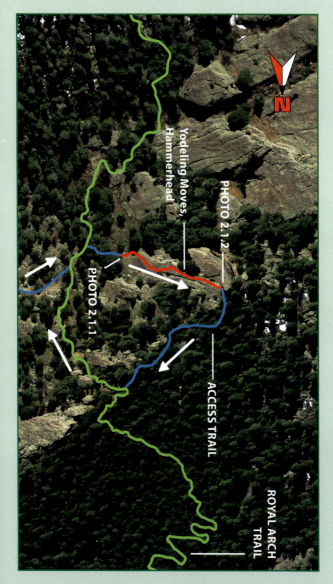

N

Yodeling Moves, Hammerhead

PHOTO 2.1.2

PHOTO 2.1.1

ACCESS TRAIL

ROYAL ARCH TRAIL

2.2 El Camino Royale (Class 4 variation start), the Regency and East Face, Royal Arch

ROUND-TRIP DISTANCE	3.4 miles
ELEVATION GAIN	1,320 feet
CLASS	4
SCRAMBLE LENGTH	900 feet
ROUND-TRIP TIME	2 hours 10 minutes
DIFFICULTY RANK	4 of 20
DESCENT	Downclimbs (Class 4, awkward in places)

COMMENT: This excellent route combines El Camino Royale on the Regency and the East Face of Royal Arch, resulting in a classic 900-foot Class 4 scramble. The Regency's impressive summit block offers a great view of the East Face of Royal Arch as well as the Fourth and Fifth Flatirons to the west. The East Face of Royal Arch ends on top of an impressive arch. To keep the scrambling at Class 4, the start of El Camino Royale described here is a variation to the traditional start.

APPROACH: From the Hollyberry Trailhead, turn right at the trail fork on the Skunk Connector Trail. Follow this northwest for 300 yards to the Skunk Canyon Trail. Turn left onto the Skunk Canyon Trail and follow it for 1.2 miles until it ends at the Mesa Trail. Turn right onto the Mesa Trail and follow it for 0.2 mile to where a faint access trail doubles back up the hillside. Follow the access trail 0.2 mile to the base of the formation. Along the way, the access trail will pass a talus slope; stay on the access trail to the right of the talus. Close to the Regency formation, the access trail forks

Photo 2.2.1. Start of El Camino Royale.   PHOTO BY SIMON TESTA

at a boulder; take the left fork to the base of the formation
(photo 2.2.1).

SCRAMBLE: Gain the rock (photo 2.2.1) and head up the far-left
edge and within five feet of the ridge edge for 145 feet. When
a steep section is ahead, traverse left into a water gully/corner
system. Follow the corner system up a step, which is a con-
tinuation of the steep section that was avoided by traversing
left. Scramble on great holds over several steeper sections to
stay close to the corner system. The top of the corner system
is marked by a rounded juniper tree. Scramble through the
right-side limbs of the juniper to arrive at a bowl-like ledge.
From the ledge, traverse hard right for about 30 feet, first up
a step and then along a ledge to a sloping chimney. Enter the
chimney (the crux, and hard Class 4) and then scramble up a
65-foot slab to the left to a ledge. Cross the ledge to the final
section of the Regency. Scramble 160 feet up the last section

Photo 2.2.2. Start of East Face, Royal Arch.   PHOTO BY SIMON TESTA

to the impressive summit of the Regency by staying to the far right edge of the face.

Downclimb directly west, just right of the summit apex, to a ledge at the top of a sloping section of rock. The downclimb is very exposed but easy. Alternatively, you can downclimb the route for 20 feet and head left around a corner to the sloping section of rock. Head down the sloping section to an awkward step; sitting face-out on the edge seems to be the best way to cross the gap. Turn 180 degrees and head down a sloping ramp. Hike 10 feet north and then head into a cave-like slot to the left. The East Face of Royal Arch will be visible once you emerge from the slot (photo 2.2.2). Scramble 120 feet straight up the first piece of the East Face to a ledge. Continue on to the final piece of the East Face, and scramble 180 feet to the top of the arch.

Toward the top of the East Face, the easiest path is on its right side. From the top of the arch there is a great view of the summit of the Regency to the east.

Downclimb the East Face until you reach hiking terrain to the south. Hike up a bit to stand under the arch! From here, take the Royal Arch Trail down 0.15 mile to a wooden fence on the right. Head right between a gap in the fence on the access trail to Woods Quarry in 0.2 mile. From Woods Quarry head 20 yards north to a trail junction and turn right onto the Woods Quarry Trail. Follow the Woods Quarry Trail downslope for 240 yards to reach the Mesa Trail. Turn right on the Mesa Trail and then immediately left onto the Kohler Mesa Trail. Follow the Kohler Mesa Trail for 0.4 mile and at a trail junction turn right onto the Skunk Canyon Spur Trail. After 0.1 mile, turn right to stay on the Skunk Canyon Spur Trail and follow it for 0.1 mile to reach the Skunk Canyon Trail. Turn left onto the Skunk Canyon Trail and retrace your path to the Hollyberry Trailhead.

ROYAL ARCH TRAIL

ACCESS TRAIL

El Camino Royale, The Regency

East Face, Royal Arch

PHOTO 2.2.2

PHOTO 2.2.1

2.3 East Face South Side, Fifth Flatiron

ROUND-TRIP DISTANCE	3.6 miles
ELEVATION GAIN	1,800 feet
CLASS	5.5
SCRAMBLE LENGTH	500 feet
ROUND-TRIP TIME	2 hours
DIFFICULTY RANK	20 of 20
DESCENT	Downclimb (5.3) or rappel

COMMENT: East Face South Side is a 500-foot classic scramble and the **hardest scramble** in the guide. It includes several cruxes and very exposed moves and a stunning north ridge leading to a pointed summit. It is possible to rappel from the summit rappel anchor, but a downclimb is described here as the descent.

APPROACH: From the Hollyberry Trailhead, turn right at the trail fork on the Skunk Connector Trail. Follow this northwest for 300 yards to the Skunk Canyon Trail. Turn left onto the Skunk Canyon Trail and follow it for 0.4 mile to the junction with the Skunk Canyon Spur Trail. Turn right onto the Skunk Canyon Spur Trail. After 0.1 mile, at a junction, turn left to stay on the Skunk Canyon Spur Trail. After 0.1 mile turn left onto the Kohler Mesa Trail and continue 0.4 mile to its end at the Mesa Trail. Turn right onto the Mesa Trail and then immediately left onto the Woods Quarry Trail. Follow the Woods Quarry Trail for 240 yards to where it meets a trail heading north and south. Turn left toward Woods Quarry, and at the far southern end of the quarry, head uphill and west (right) on an access trail. After 0.2 mile the access trail meets the Royal Arch Trail at a wooden fence. Turn left on

Photo 2.3.1. Start of East Face South Side. PHOTO BY SIMON TESTA

the Royal Arch Trail and follow it for 0.2 mile to the Royal Arch. From here, head west without going through the arch, over a fallen barkless tree and some boulders, and head 80 yards west uphill, to the south of some flatironettes, to an alcove at the base of the Fifth Flatiron's east face. Start at the far left edge of the east face behind a tree (photo 2.3.1).

SCRAMBLE: Once on the rock (photo 2.3.1) follow the face on its south side for 180 feet to an up-to-the-left angled ledge/crack. Follow the ledge left and continue up the south side of the face to a larger ledge. The face steepens here and has some exposed slabby 5.5 moves (crux). The angle eases after the crux section where there is a large ledge. From the ledge head 20 feet right (north) to gain the incredible north ridge. Hand traverse 90 feet up the north ridge to the pointed summit.

To descend, you can rappel 75 feet north to the ground from the summit rappel anchor. Or head back down the north ridge for 90 feet to a notch and find a hole south of the notch. Lower yourself down through the hole to a slab below.

Thin Tree

Photo 2.3.2. East Face South Side downclimb. Photo by Simon Testa

Traverse the slab to where the angle steepens by a thin tree (photo 2.3.2). Downclimb an overhanging wall on the tree's south side, on small but positive holds (5.3), to a ledge 10 feet above the ground. Head west from the ledge to the ground. Follow an access trail south around the top of the Fifth Flatiron and then steeply down its south side back to the alcove at the base of the east face. From here, retrace the approach route to the Hollyberry Trailhead.

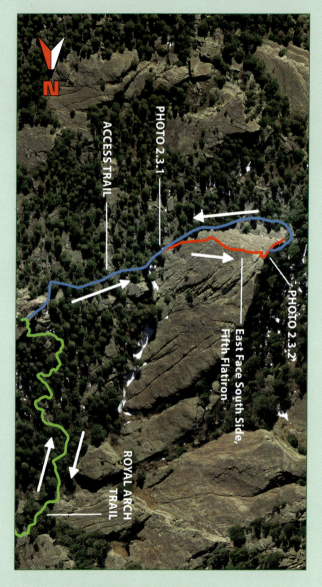

ACCESS TRAIL

PHOTO 2.3.1

PHOTO 2.3.2

East Face South Side,
Fifth Flatiron

ROYAL ARCH
TRAIL

2.4 Buckets, Amoeboid

ROUND-TRIP DISTANCE	3.7 miles
ELEVATION GAIN	1,610 feet
CLASS	4
SCRAMBLE LENGTH	300 feet
ROUND-TRIP TIME	1 hour 50 minutes
DIFFICULTY RANK	2 of 20
DESCENT	Walk off

COMMENT: Buckets on the Amoeboid is a novel Class 4 scramble with perfect hand-sized pockets (the buckets) for much of the route. The buckets make most of the scramble feel like a rock ladder. This is one of the easiest scrambles in the guide and following the buckets provides straightforward route finding.

APPROACH: From the Hollyberry Trailhead, turn right at the trail fork on the Skunk Connector Trail. Follow this northwest for 300 yards to the Skunk Canyon Trail. Turn left onto the Skunk Canyon Trail and follow it for 0.4 mile to the junction with the Skunk Canyon Spur Trail. Turn right onto the Skunk Canyon Spur Trail. After 0.1 mile, at a junction, turn left to stay on the Skunk Canyon Spur Trail. After 0.1 mile turn left onto the Kohler Mesa Trail and continue 0.4 mile to its end at the Mesa Trail. Turn right onto the Mesa Trail and then immediately left onto the Woods Quarry Trail. Follow the Woods Quarry Trail for 240 yards to where it meets a trail heading north and south. Turn left toward Woods Quarry, and at the far southern end of the quarry head uphill and west (right) on an access trail. After 0.2 mile the access trail meets the Royal Arch Trail at a wooden fence. Turn left on the Royal Arch Trail and follow it for 0.2 mile to the Royal

Photo 2.4.1 Start of Buckets.

PHOTO BY SIMON TESTA

Arch. From here, head west without going through the arch, over a fallen barkless tree and some boulders. Here, head west uphill about 50 feet and then follow a faint access trail south (left) for 0.1 mile across the hillside to the northern edge of the Amoeboid. The trail intersects the Amoeboid formation along its northern edge. From here, head down along the northern edge to the start of the scramble at the base of the formation (photo 2.4.1).

SCRAMBLE: Start the scramble between two obvious water grooves. The groove to the right has a tree growing out of it (photo 2.4.1). Scramble up and slightly right on fantastic buckets. When the pockets start to run out, head left on a rising traverse toward the left water groove. Still right of the left water groove, head up into a large vegetated gash.

At the end of the gash, head south (left) to intersect a faint access trail that follows the southern edge of the Amoeboid formation back to the start of the scramble. From here retrace the approach route to the Hollyberry Trailhead.

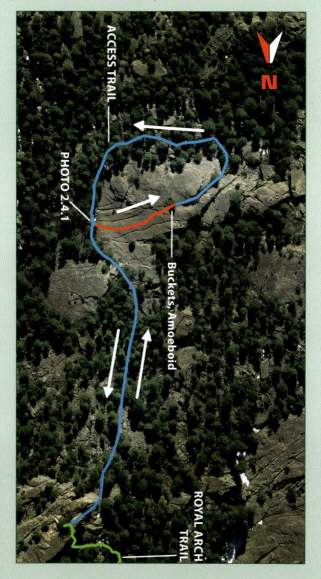

ACCESS TRAIL

PHOTO 2.4.1

Buckets, Amoeboid

ROYAL ARCH TRAIL

2.5 Regency/Royal Arch/ Hammerhead Link-up

ROUND-TRIP DISTANCE	3.7 miles
ELEVATION GAIN	1,580 feet
CLASS	4 to 5.0
SCRAMBLE LENGTH	1,300 feet
ROUND-TRIP TIME	2 hours 30 minutes
DESCENT	Refer to individual scrambles

LINK-UP			
FORMATIONS	ROUTES	CLASS	SCRAMBLE LENGTH
The Regency/ Royal Arch	El Camino Royale/ East Face	4	900 feet
Hammerhead	Yodeling Moves	5.0	400 feet

COMMENT: This excellent link-up tours 1,300 feet of easy scrambling and includes the wonderful summit of the Regency, sitting atop the Royal Arch, and a steep rising traverse to the summit of the Hammerhead. All three classic scrambles have fun downclimbs. Refer to the section overview map for the location of the individual scrambles.

APPROACH: Follow the approach for El Camino Royale, the Regency/East Face, Royal Arch (Section 2.2).

SCRAMBLE: Follow the description for El Camino Royale, the Regency/East Face, Royal Arch (Section 2.2). After descending Royal Arch, follow the Royal Arch Trail north for 0.2 mile. The short uphill hike (25 yards) to the start of the Hammerhead starts 20 yards before a wooden fence on the right. From here, follow the Yodeling Moves description (Section 2.1).

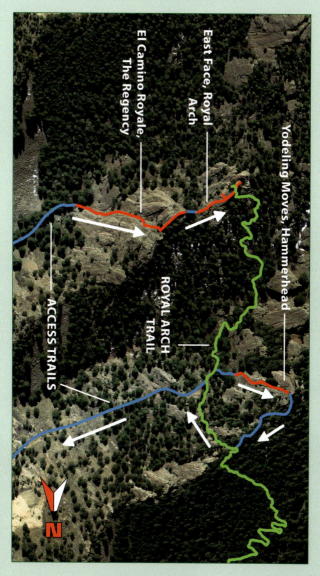

El Camino Royale,
The Regency

East Face, Royal
Arch

Yodeling Moves, Hammerhead

ACCESS TRAILS

ROYAL ARCH
TRAIL

N

Buzz Burrell, Brian Crim and Sonia Buckley on Stairway to Heaven.

NCAR TRAILHEAD

COMMENT: The seven scrambles and two scramble link-ups in this section leave from the NCAR Trailhead and include over 7,600 feet of scrambling. Two of the scrambles ascend impressive ridges that rise majestically north out of Skunk Canyon, and the other five are on Dinosaur Mountain.

The first link-up ascends Ridge One, the Amoeboid, and the Fifth Flatiron for 2,000 feet of superb scrambling. The second includes 1,195 feet of easy scrambling on Dinosaur Mountain. Refer to the NCAR Trailhead overview map for the location of the individual scrambles.

Emir Dedic on Angel's Way, Ridge Three.   PHOTO BY SIMON TESTA

GETTING THERE: To reach the NCAR Trailhead, turn west on Table Mesa Drive from the intersection of Broadway and Table Mesa Drive. Follow Table Mesa Drive for 1.3 miles where Table Mesa Drive turns into NCAR Road. NCAR Road is open to the public between 6 a.m. and 10 p.m. Continue on NCAR Road for 1.2 miles. Park in the NCAR parking lot.

Simon Testa and John Christie on Angel's Way.   PHOTO BY KEVIN SMITH

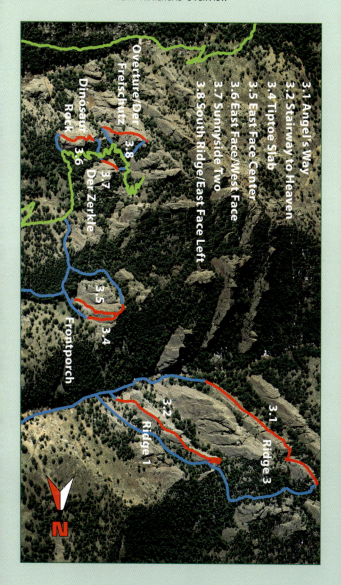

3.1 Angel's Way
3.2 Stairway to Heaven
3.4 Tiptoe Slab
3.5 East Face Center
3.6 East Face/West Face
3.7 Sunnyside Two
3.8 South Ridge/East Face Left

Overture/Der
Freischutz

Dinosaur
Rock

3.8

3.6

3.7

Der Zerkle

3.5

3.4

Frontporch

3.2

Ridge 1

3.1

Ridge 3

N

3.1 Angel's Way, Ridge Three

SEASONAL CLOSURE	February 1 to July 31 (see page 12)
ROUND-TRIP DISTANCE	2.9 miles
ELEVATION GAIN	1,780 feet
CLASS	5.1
SCRAMBLE LENGTH	1,400 feet
ROUND-TRIP TIME	2 hours
DIFFICULTY RANK	12 of 20
DESCENT	Downclimb (5.0)

COMMENT: Angel's Way is an outstanding route and is the author's favorite Flatirons scramble. It follows a ridgeline for an impressive 1,400 feet and is the longest individual scramble in this guide. The scramble is mostly Class 4 but contains the occasional cruxy 5.1 step. The summit features fantastic views of the Hippo Head to the north and the ridges rising out of Skunk Canyon to the south.

APPROACH: From the NCAR Trailhead, take one of the parallel Walter Orr Roberts Trails west (toward the Flatirons) for 0.2 mile along the NCAR mesa. Follow the NCAR Trail off the south side of the mesa to a broad saddle, then up to a water tank after another 0.3 mile. Pass the water tank and continue downhill for 0.1 mile to a trail fork. Take the right fork and continue 200 yards to join the Mesa Trail. Follow the Mesa Trail north, crossing a wooden bridge over Skunk Canyon Creek, and continue west up steps. After 120 yards the Mesa Trail turns north (right). Instead of heading north, continue straight past a small wall up Skunk Canyon on an access trail with great views of the Backporch and Satan's Slab. After 125 yards, at a large pine tree, continue up Skunk Canyon. From here the access trail route is difficult to describe, but you

Photo 3.1.1. Start of Angel's Way.

should follow Skunk Canyon, avoiding the steeper sections of the drainage. The trail switches back and forth across the creek but stays along the creek. The approach passes the start of Stairway to Heaven (Section 3.2), when the trail reaches a portion of the creek that runs down terraced rock steps, which is about 300 yards from a large pine tree. From here, continue up the creek, initially on its south side and then along the creek. Just past where Ridge Two rises out of the canyon, after 100 yards, you'll reach large boulders. Follow the trail north in front of the boulders and climb up an awkward slot containing a deciduous tree with a slab on its right. Continue to follow the access trail across rocks (not up the drainage), then steeply up with the south side of Ridge Two close on the right. Ridge Three is the next rock ridge after

Photo 3.1.2. Emir Dedic on Angel's Way downclimb.

Ridge Two ends and is 150 yards after the boulders. Photo 3.1.1 shows the start of the scramble.

SCRAMBLE. Start the scramble just up from a tree and head up a diagonal weakness to the ridge (photo 3.1.1). Stay on or very close to the ridge. After about 370 feet, step over an odd-shaped tree that is growing out of the east side of the ridge and bends over the ridgetop. Behind the tree there is a vertical step that is gained on the east side of the ridge. Continue up a small face (5.1) and back to the main ridge. After 160 feet of a less steep section, there is an impressive slab with a layback crack. Climb the layback crack toward a ledge with trees. Shortly after the trees, step across a notch, then climb a short steep section with good holds to reach the next step in the ridge. Climb on to the step (5.1) and then up a small steep face on the eastern side of the ridge. Continue up the ridge on easy terrain to the next step. Climb the step using good handholds at eye level (5.0). Continue to the summit of the main piece of Angel's Way after 1,000 feet of total scrambling.

Descend from the summit via a groove with a tree. Continue along a ledge to hiking territory. From here it is a short hike to the next piece of rock. Gain this next piece behind a tree near the base of the rock. Initially the rock is lichen covered. Follow a weakness to more trees and then gain the ridge and follow it toward the final summit. The final summit is 400 feet above from the previous summit.

Downclimb by reversing the final slab, then follow a ledge and hand traverse to the north. Follow the path of least resistance down over rocks into a groove and then downclimb a slot/notch (5.0) to the ground (photo 3.1.2). From here, hike north a short distance toward the impressive Hippo Head formation. Then head east through a tunnel-like cave between boulders. Continue downhill on a faint access trail that passes the south side of the Amoeboid formation on the left after about 150 yards. Just as the east face of Amoeboid becomes visible, turn right and traverse the hillside without losing elevation. A faint access trail exists across the hillside, but it is easy to miss. Follow this trail or bushwhack for 100 yards to reach a gap between the Hobo on the left and Ridge One on the right. Pass through a gap between these formations. This is a good opportunity to check out the downclimb from Stairway to Heaven from the bottom (photo 3.2.2). Take an access trail down a steep and loose gully with Ridge One on the right and Hilly Billy Ridge on the left. Follow this gully all the way back down to Skunk Canyon. The trail starts close to Ridge One and then crosses the gully and is close to Hilly Billy Ridge for most of the descent back to Skunk Canyon. When you reach Skunk Canyon (near the start of Stairway to Heaven), retrace the approach route to the NCAR Trailhead.

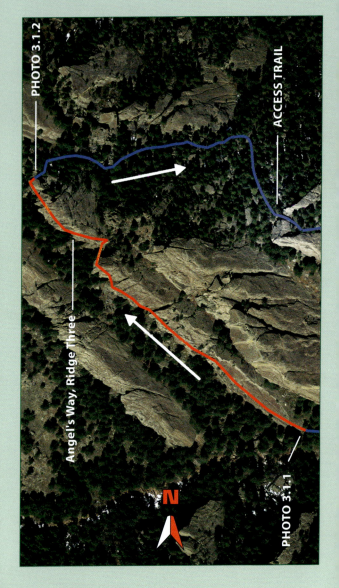

PHOTO 3.1.2

ACCESS TRAIL

Angel's Way, Ridge Three

N

PHOTO 3.1.1

3.2 Stairway to Heaven, Ridge One

ROUND-TRIP DISTANCE	2.2 miles
ELEVATION GAIN	1,340 feet
CLASS	5.3
SCRAMBLE LENGTH	1,200 feet
ROUND-TRIP TIME	1 hour 50 minutes
DIFFICULTY RANK	15 of 20
DESCENT	Downclimb (5.2) or rappel

COMMENT: Stairway to Heaven is an absolute Flatirons classic. The first pitch contains the hardest scrambling and an exposed 5.3 crux, but the rest of the route is Class 4 to 5.0. A short side excursion to the super impressive summit of Like Heaven (5.3) is possible en route. The scramble involves some hiking between sections of rock, but this detracts only slightly from this excellent scramble. At 1,200 feet, this is the second longest individual scramble in the guide. A short rappel is possible from a tree at the end of the scramble, but a cruxy 5.2 downclimb is described here.

APPROACH: From the NCAR Trailhead, take one of the parallel Walter Orr Roberts Trails west (toward the Flatirons) for 0.2 mile along the NCAR mesa. Follow the NCAR Trail off the south side of the mesa to a broad saddle, then up to a water tank after another 0.3 mile. Pass the water tank and continue downhill for 0.1 mile to a trail fork. Take the right fork and continue 200 yards to join the Mesa Trail. Follow the Mesa Trail north, crossing a wooden bridge over Skunk Canyon Creek, and continue west up steps. After 120 yards the Mesa Trail turns north (right). Instead of heading north, continue straight past a small wall up Skunk Canyon on an access trail with great views of the Backporch and Satan's Slab. After 125

Photo 3.2.1. Start of Stairway to Heaven.   PHOTO BY SIMON TESTA

yards, at a large pine tree, continue up Skunk Canyon. The
trail switches back and forth over the creek and travels along
the creek in places. Look right after about 300 yards when
the trail reaches a portion of the creek that runs down terraced rock steps. Stairway to Heaven, the ridge of rock before
the impressive face of Satan's Slab, starts here (photo 3.2.1).

SCRAMBLE: Follow the rock slab out of Skunk Canyon up into a
left-facing corner system (5.1) heading toward an overhang
at 140 feet (photo 3.2.1). Bypass the overhang by making an
exposed traverse left, then up. This is the crux (5.3) of the
route. From here, head up and right to gain the main piece
of rock. Scramble for 320 feet along the ridge to reach a short
hike over to the next piece of rock. Gain the next piece via a
steep wall to the main face and scramble 190 feet to a notch
that separates the spectacular Like Heaven summit from the
main piece of the rock. The summit of Like Heaven (5.3) is a
worthy side excursion; if you scramble to this summit, reverse
your course back to the notch. Continue 420 feet to the summit of Stairway to Heaven, staying close to the ridge edge.

Photo 3.2.2. Emir Dedic on Stairway to Heaven downclimb.

From the summit, scramble north along a short knife-edge ridge and then east down a left-facing corner to a ledge (it is also possible to do a 60-foot rappel east from a tree. Find the tree by continuing north after the knife-edge). The down-climb after the left-facing corner is awkward and somewhat lichen covered (photo 3.2.2). Descend a right-facing corner until it is possible to step north onto a short ramp. From here, avoid the lichen-covered slab directly below by heading a few feet north to a right-facing shallow corner. Take this to the ground. From the base of the downclimb, take an access trail down a steep and loose gully with Ridge One on the right and Hilly Billy Ridge on the left. Follow this gully all the way back to Skunk Canyon. The trail starts close to Ridge One and then crosses the gully and is close to Hilly Billy Ridge for most of the descent back to Skunk Canyon. When you reach Skunk Canyon near the start of Stairway to Heaven, retrace the approach route to the NCAR Trailhead.

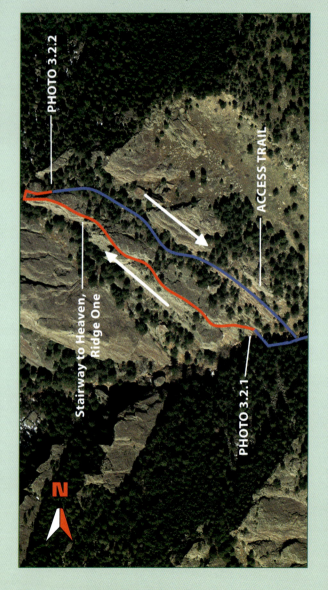

PHOTO 3.2.2

ACCESS TRAIL

Stairway to Heaven,
Ridge One

PHOTO 3.2.1

3.3 Stairway to Heaven/Buckets/ East Face South Side Link-up

ROUND-TRIP DISTANCE	3.1 miles
ELEVATION GAIN	1,830 feet
CLASS	4 to 5.5
SCRAMBLE LENGTH	2,000 feet
ROUND-TRIP TIME	3 hours 10 minutes
DESCENT	Refer to individual scrambles

LINK-UP			
FORMATIONS	**ROUTES**	**CLASS**	**SCRAMBLE LENGTH**
Ridge One	Stairway to Heaven	5.3	1,200 feet
Amoeboid	Buckets	4	300 feet
Fifth Flatiron	East Face South Side	5.5	500 feet

COMMENT: This outstanding link-up tours 2,000 feet of high quality rock. Due to the inclusion of the hardest scramble in the guide (East Face South Side) and the 5.3 crux move on Stairway to Heaven, this is the hardest link-up in the guide. Refer to the section overview map for the location of the individual scrambles.

APPROACH: Follow the approach for Stairway to Heaven, Ridge One (Section 3.2).

SCRAMBLE: Follow the description for Stairway to Heaven (Section 3.2). After descending from Stairway to Heaven, hike north between a gap between Stairway to Heaven and the adjacent formation, the Hobo. Traverse the hillside without losing elevation on a faint access trial. After 100 yards of traversing, you'll reach the Ameoboid formation. Descend slightly to the base of the Amoeboid. From here, follow the description for Buckets (Section 2.4). But instead of scrambling up into a large vegetated gash near the top of Buckets, traverse right (north) just before the gash to the north edge of the Amoeboid. From here, scramble down a short groove to the ground. Here, traverse the hillside for 120 yards to the southern edge of the Fifth Flatiron, passing the base of the tree-covered Hourglass formation en route. From here, follow the East Face South Side description (Section 2.3).

The descent differs from East Face South Side. After descending the access trail from the Fifth Flatiron, instead of following the Royal Arch Trail from the Royal Arch, head down a faint access trail to the south (right) of Royal Arch for 0.3 mile to the Mesa Trail. The trail passes the southern edge and the base of the Regency formation en route to the Mesa Trail. Turn right on the Mesa Trail and follow it for 250 yards past the Skunk Canyon Trail junction. Continue on the Mesa Trail for 0.3 mile to a point by a small wall where the access trail turned off for the start Stairway to Heaven. From here, retrace the approach route to the NCAR Trailhead.

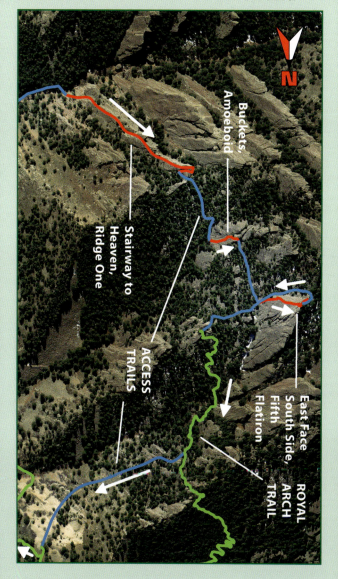

Buckets, Amoeboid

Stairway to Heaven, Ridge One

ACCESS TRAILS

East Face South Side, Fifth Flatiron

ROYAL ARCH TRAIL

3.4 Tiptoe Slab, Frontporch

ROUND-TRIP DISTANCE	2.1 miles
ELEVATION GAIN	980 feet
CLASS	5.3
SCRAMBLE LENGTH	400 feet
ROUND-TRIP TIME	1 hour 20 minutes
DIFFICULTY RANK	18 of 20
DESCENT	Downclimb (awkward 5.0)

COMMENT: Tiptoe Slab is an aptly named 400-foot scramble that has sustained Class 5.3 sections. Due to its slabby nature and the potential to stray off-route into more difficult territory, this classic route feels more serious than most of the routes in this guide. Fantastic views of the Backporch to the west and the impressive ridges rising from Skunk Canyon to the north are available from the summit.

APPROACH: From the NCAR Trailhead, take one of the parallel Walter Orr Roberts Trails west (toward the Flatirons) for 0.2 mile along the NCAR mesa. Follow the NCAR Trail off the south side of the mesa to a broad saddle, then up to a water tank after another 0.3 mile. Pass the water tank and continue downhill for 0.1 mile to a trail fork. Take the left fork and continue 0.1 mile to the junction with the Mesa and Mallory Cave trails. Go straight across the Mesa Trail at the junction onto the Mallory Cave Trail. Continue on the Mallory Cave Trail for 0.1 mile to a climbing access trail that joins from the right 75 yards after the Mallory Cave Trail crosses a drainage. Follow the climbing access trail for 0.2 mile to reach the base of the Frontporch. Follow the climbing access trail north along the base of the Frontporch for 60 yards to the start of the scramble (photo 3.4.1).

Photo 3.4.1. Start of Tiptoe Slab.

PHOTO BY SIMON TESTA

SCRAMBLE: The scramble ascends an east-facing slab with a right-facing corner on its left side and a left-facing corner on its right side. Start the scramble just right of the right-facing corner (photo 3.4.1). Look carefully for a bolt 70 feet above. Head straight up toward the bolt, and when you reach it, trend slightly right to stay on easier terrain. Continue upward, meandering slightly right or left, to stay on the easiest line toward the summit. Near the top of the face, head left and scramble up past a tree and the final section of rock to the summit. Head south (left) along the summit area toward a dead tree.

For the downclimb, head down from the tree and climb along a diagonal ramp/ledge (photo 3.4.2). Step over a pillar/

Mini Arch

Photo 3.4.2. Frontporch downclimb.

PHOTO BY SIMON TESTA

mini arch of rock and traverse down the ledge (awkward 5.0). Traverse down the ramp with hands on good holds and feet on a sloping ramp. Once off the rock, follow the access trail down to the base of the Frontporch. From here, retrace the approach route to the NCAR Trailhead.

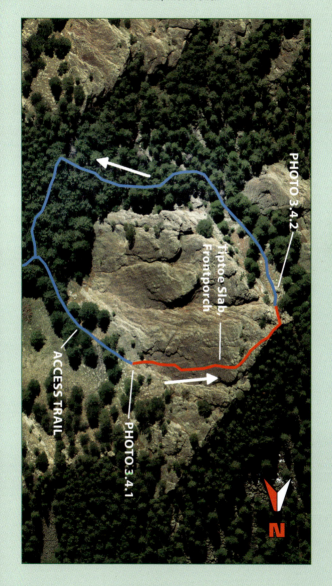

PHOTO 3.4.2

Tiptoe Slab,
Frontporch

ACCESS TRAIL

PHOTO 3.4.1

N

3.5 East Face Center, Frontporch

ROUND-TRIP DISTANCE	2.1 miles
ELEVATION GAIN	980 feet
CLASS	5.0
SCRAMBLE LENGTH	500 feet
ROUND-TRIP TIME	1 hour 15 minutes
DIFFICULTY RANK	10 of 20
DESCENT	Downclimb (awkward 5.0)

COMMENT: East Face Center is a fantastic 500-foot 5.0 scramble and is the author's favorite Dinosaur Mountain scramble. The downclimb is the crux at an awkward 5.0. The summit has spectacular views of the Backporch to the west and the impressive ridges rising from Skunk Canyon to the north.

APPROACH: From the NCAR Trailhead, take one of the parallel Walter Orr Roberts Trails west (toward the Flatirons) for 0.2 mile along the NCAR mesa. Follow the NCAR Trail off the south side of the mesa to a broad saddle, then up to a water tank after another 0.3 mile. Pass the water tank and continue downhill for 0.1 mile to a fork in the trail. Take the left fork and continue 0.1 mile to the junction with the Mesa and Mallory Cave Trails. Go straight at the junction onto the Mallory Cave Trail. Continue on the Mallory Cave Trail for 0.1 mile to a climbing access trail that joins from the right 75 yards after the Mallory Cave Trail crosses a drainage. Follow the climbing access trail for 0.2 mile to reach the base of the Frontporch. Follow the climbing access trail north along base of the Frontporch for 20 yards to the start of the scramble (photo 3.5.1).

SCRAMBLE: Start just left of a rib with left-facing corner (photo 3.5.1). Scramble up and within 20 feet of the rib. When you

Photo 3.5.1. Start of East Face Center.

are level with the top of the rib, traverse right and up, then directly up toward a bulge. Before reaching the bulge, traverse right and then left up a diagonal weakness. Gain the bulge and traverse right for 10 feet into a depression to avoid a steeper section above. Continue straight up, staying south (left) and within 10 feet of a groove (the groove can also be climbed at Class 4). As the scrambling difficulty eases, climb past a tree and up the final section of rock to the summit. Head south (left) along the summit area toward a dead tree.

For the downclimb, head down from the tree and climb along a diagonal ramp/ledge (photo 3.4.2). Step over a pillar/mini-arch of rock and traverse down the ledge (awkward 5.0). Traverse down the ramp with hands on good holds and feet on a sloping ramp. Once off the rock, follow the access trail back to the base of the Frontporch. From here, retrace the approach route to the NCAR Trailhead.

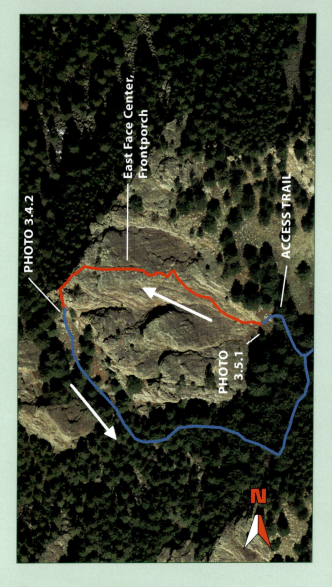

East Face Center,
Frontporch

ACCESS TRAIL

PHOTO 3.4.2

PHOTO
3.5.1

3.6 East Face/West Face, Dinosaur Rock

ROUND-TRIP DISTANCE	2.5 miles
ELEVATION GAIN	940 feet
CLASS	5.4
SCRAMBLE LENGTH	295 feet
ROUND-TRIP TIME	1 hour 30 minutes
DIFFICULTY RANK	19 of 20
DESCENT	Downclimb West Face (Class 4)

COMMENT: The East Face is an excellent classic scramble. Including the West Face downclimb, it is 295 feet. Most of the scramble is Class 4 or 5.0, with the exception of an exposed and awkward 5.4 crux that bypasses a small overhang. The awkwardness and exposure of the crux makes this one of the hardest scrambles in this guide.

APPROACH: From the NCAR Trailhead, take one of the parallel Walter Orr Roberts Trails west (toward the Flatirons) for 0.2 mile along the NCAR mesa. Follow the NCAR Trail off the south side of the mesa to a broad saddle, then up to a water tank after another 0.3 mile. Pass the water tank and continue downhill for 0.1 mile to a trail fork. Take the left fork and continue 0.1 mile to the junction with the Mesa and Mallory Cave trails. Go straight across the Mesa Trail at the junction onto the Mallory Cave Trail. After 0.5 mile the trail turns right more steeply uphill near the popular bolted climbs of Dinosaur Rock. Here, rather than heading uphill on the main trail, continue to head south (straight) for 40 yards along the base of Dinosaur Rock. Pass a large slab leaning against the front of Dinosaur Rock and then head to the start of the scramble (photo 3.6.1).

Photo 3.6.1. Start of East Face.

PHOTO BY SIMON TESTA

SCRAMBLE: Head up a rib of rock to the right of a red-colored corner and to the left of the large slab leaning against Dinosaur Rock (photo 3.6.1). After 180 feet, traverse delicately up and left on a slab (5.3) directly below a small overhang. Do not traverse early on the more difficult red-colored rock. When you reach a step in the overhang, bypass it on its left (5.4 crux) at a left-facing flake to reach a good hold. Continue straight up to the summit.

From here, descend the West Face Route (photo 3.6.2) by downclimbing a steep west-facing wall along the path of

Photo 3.6.2. Dinosaur Rock downclimb.

PHOTO BY SIMON TESTA

least resistance to a ledge. From here, head west and then south along a short ridge to another steep section. Make a descending traverse north (left when facing the rock) to the ground. From here, head north to intersect the Mallory Cave Trail. Turn right onto the Mallory Cave Trail and continue 150 yards back to just past the bolted climbs on Dinosaur Rock and retrace the approach route to the NCAR Trailhead.

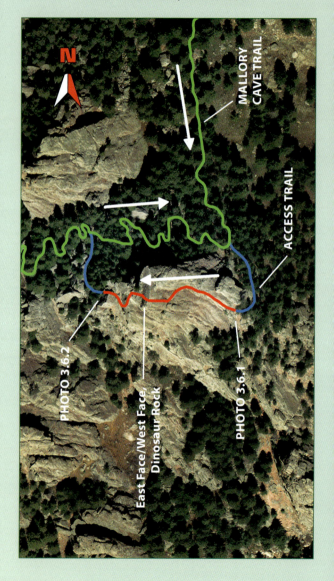

MALLORY CAVE TRAIL

ACCESS TRAIL

PHOTO 3.6.2

PHOTO 3.6.1

East Face/West Face, Dinosaur Rock

3.7 Sunnyside Two, Der Zerkle

ROUND-TRIP DISTANCE	2.6 miles
ELEVATION GAIN	1,000 feet
CLASS	4
SCRAMBLE LENGTH	200 feet
ROUND-TRIP TIME	1 hour 20 minutes
DIFFICULTY RANK	1 of 20
DESCENT	Walk off

COMMENT: Sunnyside Two is a fun and easy 200-foot Class 4 route. It is the easiest and most straightforward scramble in the guide and is recommended as the first scramble to tackle in this guide if you are new to scrambling. The top of this scramble boasts excellent views of Dinosaur Rock and Der Freischutz to the south and the Hand and Finger Flatiron to the west.

APPROACH: From the NCAR Trailhead, take one of the parallel Walter Orr Roberts Trails west (toward the Flatirons) for 0.2 mile along the NCAR mesa. Follow the NCAR Trail off the south side of the mesa to a broad saddle, and up to a water tank after another 0.3 mile. Pass the water tank and continue downhill for 0.1 mile to a trail fork. Take the left fork and continue 0.1 mile to the junction with the Mesa and Mallory Cave trails. Go straight across the Mesa Trail at the junction onto the Mallory Cave Trail. After 0.5 mile the trail passes the popular bolted climbs of Dinosaur Rock. Continue on the Mallory Cave Trail for 180 yards to reach the base of the climb by a wooden post (photo 3.7.1).

SCRAMBLE: Start directly below the obvious water groove (photo 3.7.1) and follow the easiest line up the groove on good holds. Toward the top, pass a large boulder on the left and after

Photo 3.7.1. Start of Sunnyside Two.

a ledge, scramble a Class 3 ridge-like section to the top of the route (Sunnyside Two does not go to the summit of Der Zerkle).

Hike/scramble (Class 2) down and then left to join the Mallory Cave Trail. En route go through a gap between two rocks and join the Mallory Cave Trail at the base of the Hand formation. Follow the Mallory Cave Trail down 0.7 mile to the junction with the Mesa and NCAR trails. From here, retrace the approach route to the NCAR Trailhead. You can reach the summit of Der Zerkle via the West Face (5.0) route, which is not described in this guide due to its lower quality and seasonal closures.

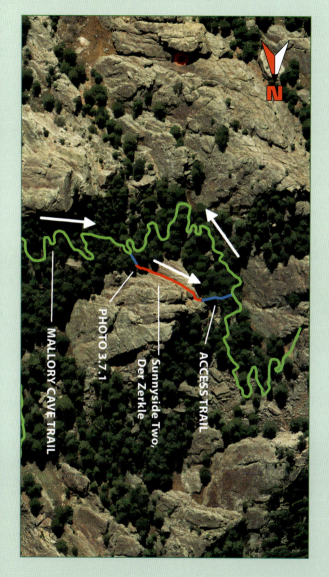

MALLORY CAVE TRAIL

PHOTO 3.7.1

Sunnyside Two,
Der Zerkle

ACCESS TRAIL

3.8 South Ridge, Overture, and East Face Left, Der Freischutz

SEASONAL CLOSURE	February 1 to July 31 (see page 12)
ROUND-TRIP DISTANCE	2.7 miles
ELEVATION GAIN	1,100 feet
CLASS	5.0
SCRAMBLE LENGTH	495 feet
ROUND-TRIP TIME	1 hour 40 minutes
DIFFICULTY RANK	8 of 20
DESCENT	Downclimb (awkward Class 4)

COMMENT: The South Ridge of Overture and East Face Left on Der Freischutz combine to form an excellent 495-foot scramble. The South Ridge is the author's favorite way to access the scrambling on Der Freischutz. An awkward 5.0 downclimb off Der Freischutz is the crux of the scramble. Great views of the Dinosaur Mountain's high concentration of impressive rock formations are available along the route and from the summit.

APPROACH: From the NCAR Trailhead, take one of the parallel Walter Orr Roberts Trails west (toward the Flatirons) for 0.2 mile along the NCAR mesa. Follow the NCAR Trail off the south side of the mesa to a broad saddle, and up to a water tank after another 0.3 mile. Pass the water tank and continue downhill for 0.1 mile to a trail fork. Take the left fork and continue 0.1 mile to the junction with the Mesa and Mallory Cave trails. Go straight across the Mesa Trail at the junction onto the Mallory Cave Trail. After 0.5 mile the trail passes the popular bolted climbs of Dinosaur Rock. Continue on the Mallory Cave Trail for 0.15 mile to

Photo 3.8.1. Simon Testa on start of South Ridge.

the Der Freischutz formation, where the trail turns to the north. Instead of following the trail to the north, head south between the base of Der Freischutz and the rock to the east. Overture is attached to the front of Der Freischutz. Continue to walk down between the rocks to the southern end of the East Face of Overture (photo 3.8.1).

SCRAMBLE: Start scrambling at the southern edge of the east face. Head straight up on great pockets, then traverse south (left) toward the exposed south ridge (photo 3.8.1). There is a short step/wall toward the top of the ridge. Traverse right onto the step and follow a groove ending in a notch to the summit of Overture. From here, scramble (Class 2) over to the east face of Der Freischutz by heading down a triangular-shaped boulder. Scramble straight up the face (photo 3.8.2) and then head up and left to follow a series of ramps. There

Photo 3.8.2. Start of East Face Left.

are two ramp systems; the one farthest to the left is easier (Class 3) than the right (Class 4). After the ramps, pass a tree and continue to the west summit of Der Freischutz.

To reach the awkward 5.0 downclimb, head back 20 feet east and then north (left) down a gully toward a large tree. Lower on good handholds and continue down a triangular shaped ramp (photo 3.8.3). Once off the rock, go down

Photo 3.8.3. Der Freischutz downclimb.

PHOTO BY SIMON TESTA

through a tight squeeze hole behind a boulder by the base of a large tree. Hike down and left, first through a slot between two rocks, and then on a faint trail and over boulders to reach the Mallory Cave Trail at the base of the Hand formation. Follow the Mallory Cave Trail 0.7 mile to the junction with the Mesa and NCAR Trails. From here, retrace the approach route to the NCAR Trailhead.

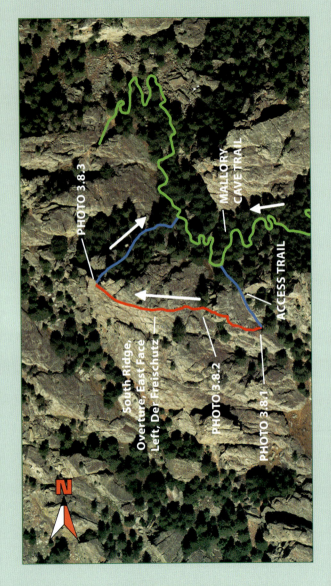

MALLORY CAVE TRAIL

PHOTO 3.8.3

ACCESS TRAIL

South Ridge,
Overture, East Face
Left, Der Freischutz

PHOTO 3.8.2

PHOTO 3.8.1

N

3.9 Dinosaur Mountain Link-up

SEASONAL CLOSURE	Der Freischutz February 1 to July 31 (refer to page 12)
ROUND-TRIP DISTANCE	3.0 miles
ELEVATION GAIN	1,700 feet
CLASS	4 to 5.0
SCRAMBLE LENGTH	1,195 feet
ROUND-TRIP TIME	2 hours 15 minutes
DESCENT	Refer to individual scrambles

LINK-UP			
FORMATIONS	**ROUTES**	**CLASS**	**SCRAMBLE LENGTH**
Frontporch	East Face Center	5.0	500 feet
Der Zerkle	Sunnyside Two	4	200 feet
Overture/Der Freischutz	South Ridge/ East Face Left	5.0	495 feet

COMMENT: This is a fun and easy 1,195-foot link-up with the difficulty not surpassing 5.0. It is the easiest link-up in the guide and includes three scrambles on Dinosaur Mountain. Refer to the section overview map for the location of the individual scrambles.

APPROACH: Follow the approach for East Face Center, Frontporch (Section 3.5).

SCRAMBLE: Start by following the description for East Face Center (Section 3.5). After scrambling the East Face Center, instead of descending on the access trail back to the base of the Frontporch, head south and up a slope (not west up a drainage) just before reaching the base of the Frontporch, after the trail crosses a rock band. As you crest the slope, the

East Gazebo formation is on the right. Continue downhill close to the East Gazebo to the Mallory Cave Trail. Turn right on the Mallory Cave Trail and continue 0.1 mile to where the trail passes the popular bolted climbs of Dinosaur Rock. From here, follow the Sunnyside Two description (Section 3.7).

After scrambling Sunnyside Two and descending to the Mallory Cave Trail by the Hand formation, continue 120 yards down the Mallory Cave Trail until the trail switchbacks left (north) by the base of Der Freischutz. Instead of heading north, continue south, following the South Ridge/East Face Left description (Section 3.8).

Matthias Messner and Angela Tomczik on Sunnyside Two.

PHOTO BY BRENDAN BLANCHARD

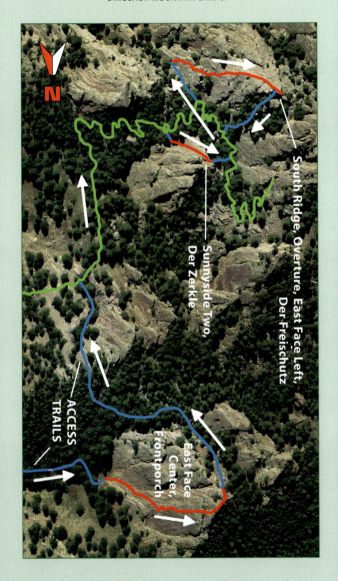

South Ridge, Overture, East Face Left, Der Freischutz

Sunnyside Two, Der Zerkle

ACCESS TRAILS

East Face Center, Frontporch

Wesley Cropp and Andrew Lainis on the Central Shanahan Crag.

CRAGMOOR TRAILHEAD

COMMENT: The three scrambles and one scramble link-up in this section all leave from the Cragmoor Trailhead and include 3,400 feet of scrambling. This trailhead sees far less use than the Chautauqua and NCAR trailheads. Diagonal on the Slab is a true Flatiron classic and is one of the three scrambles in the guide over 1,000 feet. The link-up described here combines excellent scrambles on the less-travelled Central and Northern Shanahan Crags. Refer to the Cragmoor Trailhead overview map for the location of the individual scrambles.

GETTING THERE: To reach the Cragmoor Trailhead, turn west on Table Mesa Drive from the intersection of Broadway and Table Mesa Drive. Follow Table Mesa Drive for 0.7 mile then turn left onto Lehigh Street. Follow Lehigh Street for 0.8 mile and turn right onto Cragmoor Road. The trailhead is at the end of Cragmoor Road after 0.2 mile. Parking is available along Cragmoor Road.

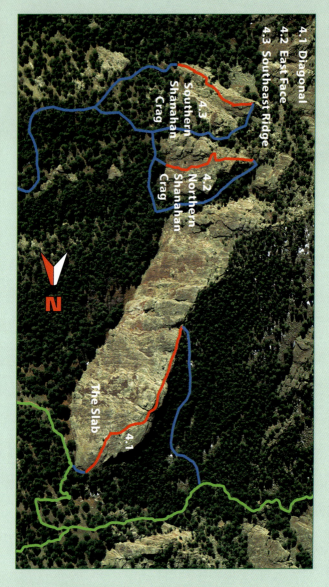

4.1 Diagonal
4.2 East Face
4.3 Southeast Ridge

Southern
Shanahan
Crag

4.3

Northern
Shanahan
Crag

4.2

N

The Slab

4.1

4.1 Diagonal (Class 4 variation start), The Slab

ROUND-TRIP DISTANCE	3.3 miles
ELEVATION GAIN	1,430 feet
CLASS	4
SCRAMBLE LENGTH	1,100 feet
ROUND-TRIP TIME	2 hours 10 minutes
DIFFICULTY RANK	6 of 20
DESCENT	Downclimb (awkward Class 4)

COMMENT: Diagonal is an outstanding 1,100-foot scramble. Due to its large horizontal expanse and excellent Class 2 and 3 ridge sections, this classic scramble has a mountaineering feel. A Class 4 variation start is described here to keep the entire scramble at Class 4 or less. The Slab's ridgeline has fantastic views of the Fern Canyon Slabs rising out of the canyon to the north.

APPROACH: From the Cragmoor Trailhead, follow the Cragmoor Connector Trail steeply uphill for 0.2 mile. At the top of the Cragmoor Connector Trail, head right on the North Fork Shanahan Trail. After 0.2 mile, at a notice board, turn right to continue on the North Fork Shanahan Trail. Continue 0.5 mile to reach the Mesa and the Shanahan/Mesa trails junction. Stay straight to join the Shanahan/Mesa Trail and continue for 0.4 mile to the base of the Slab. The trail continues to the north (right) and passes very close to the northern corner of the rock. Here, head uphill on a faint access trail along the northern edge of the rock for 30 yards to a rock ramp (photo 4.1.1).

SCRAMBLE: Scramble up a Class 4 ramp (photo 4.1.1). Alternatively, begin the route at the traditional start at the far north-

Photo 4.1.1. Joe Cavarretta, Nicklaus Combs, Eric LiPuma on start of Diagonal. PHOTO BY SIMON TESTA

ern, lowest corner of the rock at 5.3. As the ramp steepens, continue up a weakness to an odd-shaped flake. Make an exposed step (hard Class 4) across to the flake and then head straight up to a ledge. Head diagonally up and left following flakes/ledges and then head straight up at a rock protrusion that is 50 feet directly below two trees. Head up, taking the easiest line to the left tree. Behind the tree, gain a flake system by stepping left. Head straight up along the northern (right)

Photo 4.1.2. Simon Testa on Diagonal downclimb.

edge of the flake system. The flake system gets steeper toward its top and ends at a rounded juniper tree. Climb the short smooth slab directly behind the juniper and then head straight up to the summit ridge. Head left (south) straight along the ridge proper for 80 feet to a notch. At the notch, scramble

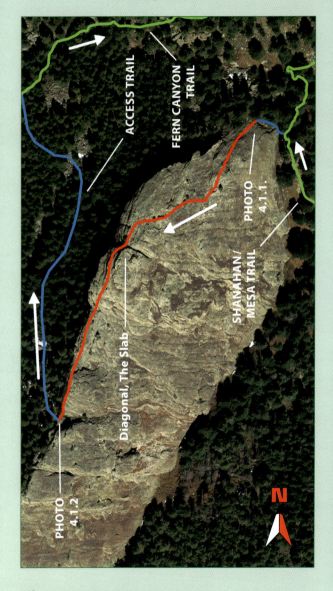

ACCESS TRAIL

FERN CANYON TRAIL

PHOTO 4.1.1.

SHANAHAN/ MESA TRAIL

Diagonal, The Slab

PHOTO 4.1.2

N

up a ramp behind a dead tree and continue along the ridge for another 500 feet. Much of this section is Class 2 and 3. At a narrower portion of the ridge that has a pine tree growing from the ground up against it, hand traverse the ridge first under the pine tree's branches and then step down (awkward Class 4) at a step in the ridge.

Once you overcome the step, look west to the ground to locate the pointed flake of the downclimb. Lower to the apex of the pointed flake and make some awkward moves, slightly to climber's right, to the ground (photo 4.1.2). Head north along the edge of the backside of the Slab to the steep bolted climbs of the Slab's north face. From here, follow an access trail to the Fern Canyon Trail. Turn right onto the Fern Canyon Trail. Continue 0.1 mile to the junction with the Shanahan/Mesa Trail. Take the Shanahan/Mesa Trail (right fork) for 0.5 mile back to the base of the Slab. From here, retrace the approach route to the Cragmoor Trailhead.

4.2 East Face, Northern Shanahan Crag

ROUND-TRIP DISTANCE	3.5 miles
ELEVATION GAIN	1,710 feet
CLASS	4
SCRAMBLE LENGTH	550 feet
ROUND-TRIP TIME	2 hours 10 minutes
DIFFICULTY RANK	5 of 20
DESCENT	Walk off

COMMENT: The East Face is an excellent, seldom-scrambled, 550-foot route. This Class 4 scramble avoids an impressive overhang that caps the East Face by first traversing directly below the overhang and then traversing back above it.

APPROACH: From the Cragmoor Trailhead, follow the Cragmoor Connector Trail steeply uphill for 0.2 mile. At the top of the Cragmoor Connector Trail head right on the North Fork Shanahan Trail. After 0.2 mile, at a notice board, turn right to continue on the North Fork Shanahan Trail. Continue 0.5 mile to reach the Mesa and Shanahan/Mesa trails junction. Head left for 0.25 mile on the Mesa Trail, first downhill to a drainage and then uphill. As the trail begins to flatten out, look for the access trail that joins on the right. Follow this access trail for 0.3 mile to large boulders. Between the boulders, look for a very faint trail that heads left (south) and contours the hillside. After 100 yards the faint trail heads up a broad ridgeline. Continue for 200 yards uphill to the base of the Northern Shanahan Crag. From here, head right (north) for 50 yards along the base of the crag to the start of the scramble (photo 4.2.1).

SCRAMBLE: Start the scramble in the center of the east-facing slab, which is capped with a large overhang (photo 4.2.1).

Photo 4.2.1. Start of East Face.

PHOTO BY SIMON TESTA

Follow the path of least resistance slightly right (north) of the slab's center for almost 300 feet to reach the large overhang. Traverse hard left just below the overhang to a slotted corner. Scramble a short, steep, west-facing wall in the corner/slot to reach the face above the overhang. Traverse hard right and gain a small step at a corner. Continue straight up the face above to reach the southern summit. Another summit is directly west, but the rock is of lower quality and therefore not recommended.

From the lower summit, downclimb a short way off the rock and hike north and then east to descend the steep gully between the Northern Shanahan Crag and the next formation to the north, the Slab. From the base of the Northern Shanahan Crag, turn right to follow the base of the formation back to the approach access trail. From here, retrace the approach route to the Cragmoor Trailhead.

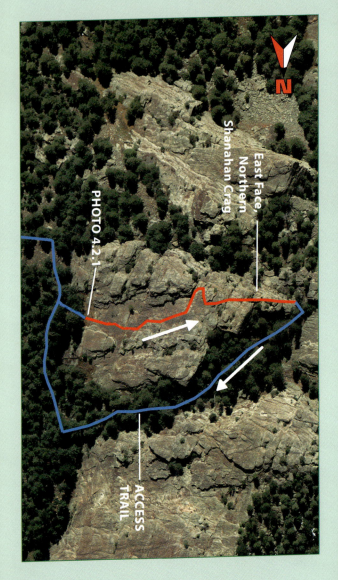

East Face,
Northern
Shanahan Crag

PHOTO 4.2.1

ACCESS
TRAIL

4.3 Southeast Ridge, Central Shanahan Crag

ROUND-TRIP DISTANCE	3.4 miles
ELEVATION GAIN	1,680 feet
CLASS	5.0
SCRAMBLE LENGTH	600 feet
ROUND-TRIP TIME	2 hours
DIFFICULTY RANK	11 of 20
DESCENT	Downclimb (Class 3)

COMMENT: The Southeast Ridge is a classic 5.0 scramble. It is less travelled than other Flatirons and as such is slightly more lichen-covered than other routes. The crux (5.0) is gaining the stepped overhang at 420 feet, but most of the scramble is Class 4. From the summit, there are impressive views of the Keel and the Devil's Wings formations to the southwest and the Sphinx formation to the south.

APPROACH: From the Cragmoor Trailhead, follow the Cragmoor Connector Trail steeply uphill for 0.2 mile. At the top of the Cragmoor Connector Trail head right on the North Fork Shanahan Trail. After 0.2 mile, at a notice board, turn right to continue on the North Fork Shanahan Trail. Continue 0.5 mile to reach the Mesa and the Shanahan/Mesa trails junction. Head left for 0.25 mile on the Mesa Trail, first downhill to a drainage and then uphill. As the trail begins to flatten out, look for the access trail that joins on the right. Follow this access trail for 0.3 mile to large boulders. Between the boulders, look for a very faint access trail that heads left (south) and contours the hillside. After 100 yards the faint access trail heads up a broad ridgeline. Continue 160 yards up the ridgeline to where you can see the top of East Shanahan Crag on the left (south).

Photo 4.3.1 Start of Southeast Ridge.

Head toward the top of the East Shanahan Crag. From the top of the East Shanahan Crag, head west for 80 yards on a very faint access trail, slightly downhill over fallen trees, and then uphill through a narrow gap between boulders to the start of the scramble (photo 4.3.1).

SCRAMBLE: Start the scramble close to the southern (left) corner of the formation (photo 4.3.1). Scramble upward, staying close to the edge of the ridge. After 120 feet, you'll reach a step that

Simon Testa, Wesley Cropp, Kevin Smith on Southeast Ridge of the
Southern Summit, Central Shanahan Crag.   PHOTO BY ANDREW LAINIS

can be avoided on its left by a very narrow ledge at the edge of
the formation. Continue up the narrow ledge to a slot between
two slabs on the right. Gain the lower slab via the slot and
then scramble up a short, steep section to gain the slab above.
Continue close to the southern edge of the formation, nego-

tiating another less steep step to reach a ledge with juniper trees, below a crack with a dead tree. Ascend the rib to the right of the tree until it is possible to gain a step on the right to reach the main portion of the rock. Continue to another step and skirt it on its right. Above, the east face is capped with a stepped overhang. Head up the center of the east face directly to the step in the overhang. You'll reach the overhang after 420 total feet of scrambling, and it is the crux of the route (5.0). Climb the step/weakness in the overhang to reach a ledge. Traverse 10 feet right on the ledge and head straight up the final face to the southern summit.

Scramble (Class 3) north and down off the formation. Hike north toward the next rock formation, Northern Shanahan Crag, and then east steeply down the gully between the Central and Northern Shanahan Crags. Initially, stay close to the north side of the northern portion of the Central Shanahan Crag, then move close to the southern edge of the Northern Shanahan Crag. Along the way you'll pass an interesting cave in the southern side of the Northern Shanahan Crag. At the base of the Northern Shanahan Crag, head downhill and slightly right (south) on a faint access trail to reach the access trail taken during the approach. From here retrace the approach route to the Cragmoor Trailhead.

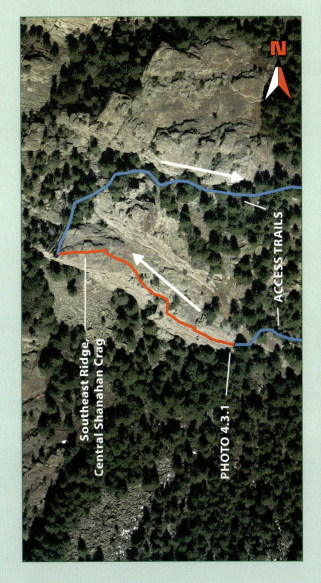

Southeast Ridge,
Central Shanahan Crag

ACCESS TRAILS

PHOTO 4.3.1

4.4 Shanahan Crags Link-up

ROUND-TRIP DISTANCE	3.6 miles
ELEVATION GAIN	2,010 feet
CLASS	4 to 5.0
SCRAMBLE LENGTH	1,150 feet
ROUND-TRIP TIME	2 hours 50 minutes
DESCENT	Refer to individual scrambles

LINK-UP			
FORMATIONS	ROUTES	CLASS	SCRAMBLE LENGTH
Central Shanahan Crag	Southeast Ridge	5.0	600 feet
Northern Shanahan Crag	East Face	4	550 feet

COMMENT: This 1,150-foot link-up combines two excellent seldom-scrambled routes. Both routes have overhangs; the Central Shanahan Crag's small stepped overhang is the route's crux (5.0), and the North Shanahan Crag's large and formidable overhang is avoided by a traverse. Refer to the section overview map for the location of the individual scrambles.

APPROACH: Follow the approach for the Southeast Ridge, Central Shanahan Crag (Section 4.3).

SCRAMBLE: Follow the description for the Southeast Ridge (Section 4.3). At the base of the Northern Shanahan Crag, after descending from the Central Shanahan Crag, instead of heading downhill on an access trail, head left (north) 50 yards to the start of the East Face of the Northern Shanahan Crag. From here, follow the East Face, Northern Shanahan description (Section 4.2).

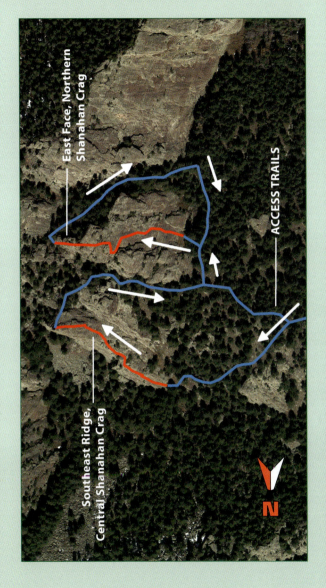

East Face, Northern Shanahan Crag

ACCESS TRAILS

Southeast Ridge, Central Shanahan Crag

N

Checklist

CHAUTAUQUA TRAILHEAD

HOLLYBERRY TRAILHEAD

NCAR TRAILHEAD

David Carner making the jump on Freeway.

About the Author

Born in England in 1971, Simon Testa grew up south of London. His passion for the outdoors began in his teenage years on a trip to the mountains of North Wales and grew during his time studying Geology at Cardiff University, Wales. After graduating with a Masters in Geology, Simon spent two seasons volunteering at Mount St. Helens National Volcanic Monument, first as an interpretive ranger and then as a climbing ranger. After moving back to the UK in 1999, he met his soon-to-be American wife, Christin, on a hiking trip in the Highlands of Scotland. Christin and Simon moved to the United States in 2000, where they continued their mutual admiration of the outdoors. They currently live in Boulder, Colorado, with their two daughters, Tilly and Eira.

Simon became a U.S. citizen in 2014 at an outdoor naturalization ceremony in Rocky Mountain National Park, overlooking his favorite mountain, Longs Peak. Simon has a deep love for Colorado and is obsessed with steep terrain and gaining elevation. In 2018, Simon gained almost 1.1 million vertical feet on foot, of which, over 235,000 feet was "on-rock" scrambling in the Flatirons. A geologist by profession, Simon is also enthusiastic about collecting, analyzing, and presenting data. This marriage between a love for the outdoors and data lead to his desire to write this guidebook.

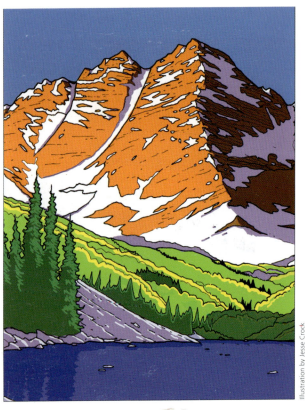

Illustration by Jesse Crock

Join Today.
Adventure Tomorrow.

The Colorado Mountain Club helps you maximize living in an
outdoor playground and connects you with other adventure-loving
mountaineers. We summit 14ers, climb rock faces, work to protect
the mountain experience and educate generations of Coloradans.